Professors as Writers

A Self-Help Guide to Productive Writing

By Robert Boice

NEW FORUMS

Stillwater, Oklahoma
U.S.A.

NEW FORUMS PRESS INC.

Published in the United States of America
by New Forums Press, Inc.1018 S. Lewis St.
Stillwater, OK 74074
www.newforums.com

Library of Congress Cataloging-in-Publication Data Pending

This book may be ordered in bulk quantities at discount from New
Forums Press, Inc., P.O. Box 876, Stillwater, OK 74076 [Federal I.D. No.
73 1123239]. Printed in the United States of America.

ISBN 10: 0-91350-713-X
ISBN 13: 978-0-913507-13-1

If you wish to be a writer, write.
Epictetus

The ink of the scholar is more sacred than the blood of the martyr.
Mohammed – *Tribute to Reason*

Foreword

PROFESSORS AS WRITERS is a self-help manual for colleagues who want to write more productively, painlessly, and successfully. It reflects my two decades of experience and research with professors as writers by compressing a lot of experience into a brief, programmatic framework.

I prepared this manual because existing books on writing problems provide only limited help for academicians facing pressures to publish. *Professors as Writers* goes beyond usual emphases on reasons why writers are unproductive (e.g., perfectionism). And it extends solutions for a lack of writing productivity past traditional ways of establishing momentum (e.g., free writing).

Specifically, *Professors as Writers* offers five innovations for facilitating productive, skillful, and successful writing. First, it presents writing problems as more than a problem of feeling stuck or afraid; writing problems occur in a spectrum including writers who write but without success or enjoyment.

Second, *Professors as Writers* conveys the structure and directedness of a successful program for unproductive writers. It does more than talk about inhibiting factors or give advice for unblocking; it directs readers through sequential steps of building insights and techniques for more efficient, effective writing.

Like the actual sessions and workshops in which I work with writers, this manual admonishes and reassures. Numerous examples of dialogs I've held with writers appear throughout the text.

Third, *Professors as Writers* presents a program for facilitating writing based on systematic research. Its components have been selected because of their proved effectiveness with large samples of academic writers. Moreover, this manual encourages readers to work on writing in systematic, measurable fashion. It includes a formal system for self-evaluations of problem tendencies across modalities (behavioral, cognitive, social) and within problem categories (e.g., procrastination).

Fourth, *Professors as Writers* combines practical and humanistic approaches for helping blocked writers cope with problems in lasting fashion. It builds in a sequence, called the Four-Step Plan, to balance various mechanisms in writing: The first step, *automaticity*, concerns ways of accessing spontaneity and creativity for writing. Automaticity sets the stage for structured forms of writing and then merges into the second step–*externality*. Externality helps ensure regular writing by finding cost-effective ways of rearranging writers' environments and, where appropriate, rewards, so that writing becomes a habitual, high priority activity. Once writers write regularly and productively, they move on to *self-control*, mastery of the self-talk (and its accompanying affect) that often undermines writing. The final step focuses on the social skills of writing; that is, ways to make writing (the process and the product) more public and more publicly supported.

Fifth, *Professors as Writers* offers individualized and flexible programs for lasting productivity and success. It represents both kinds of complexity integral to writing problems the variety of writing problems and the nonlinear nature of the writing process.

Professors as Writers is unconventional, both in content and in style. It reconceptualizes writing problems as sensible, treatable problems. It coaxes readers through a proven sequence of experiential and effective exercises. And it talks directly to readers.

Table of Contents

Introduction

Anyone whose writing has been hindered by distractions, self- doubts, procrastination, and rejections, knows about writing problems. They can act openly to delay the onset or completion of writing. They can act subtly to make writing unnecessarily painful and inefficient. And, when given free rein, writing problems can become pathological: Writing projects acquire aversive, even phobic, qualities while writers grow distressed, even depressed.

These observations may seem obvious. Yet, knowledge about writing problems is not common sense; most of us know little about them beyond our own experiences. Perhaps we've heard a few self-conscious jokes about writing blocks or, worse yet, anecdotes about writers who unblocked themselves by, say, sharpening pencils. In my two decades of experience with professors as writers, I've consistently seen people whose inexperience in discussing their blocks exceeded their shyness for revealing almost anything else, even sexual dysfunctions. They often came for help believing themselves to be unique as problem writers. And they worried that asking for help was an admission of weakness. Why is so common a problem so widely kept a secret? The answer seems to lie in the ways writing is typically taught and practiced. Only a handful of the thousands of writers I've surveyed recalled a useful and encouraging education in writing. Fewer still remembered writing teachers who didn't delight in perfectionism and criticism. None remembered much about learning to write beyond classroom assignments, especially in painless, efficient fashion. And, finally, none recalled discussions about dealing with writing problems.

Not all the blame belongs to teachers. Few of us were *forced* to write in private, without the chance to get help from more experienced writers. Few of us have been restrained from complaining or asking advice. Few of us were made to do our writing at the last minute, amidst fatigue and dissatisfaction.

The important thing, however, is to move beyond blame to accepting responsibility for getting ourselves out of the writing problems we've helped create.

Colleagues sometimes assume that my interest in writing problems came from finding solutions to my own. Not really. It started, instead, because I wrote fluently; I enjoy writing almost as much as I do talking about it. Colleagues with writing problems simply gravitated to me, apparently because of my willingness to discuss writing. What began as casual coaching to help a few friends survive the publish-or-perish rule of universities evolved into a much larger, formal program.

Once I realized what I was undertaking, I looked for direction in the literature on writing problems. It seemed exotic but unhelpful.[1] So I experimented, at first with simple techniques like having a blocked writer describe what he or she would write about if the block were magically removed. In the next meeting, I produced a typed transcript of their descriptions that I had surreptitiously recorded. And, then, we began by rewriting that. This technique worked beautifully to get writers started, but it annoyed many of them. I stopped "bugging" people.

I decided to try helping writers with a mixture of sympathetic advice and scientific scrutiny. I asked them to be research subjects in projects designed to see what techniques worked most efficiently. I collected lots of data.[2] And I discarded more techniques, some of them favorites like sensitivity groups. Eventually, I settled into a program that includes four basic stages: 1) establishing momentum and ideas with unself-conscious techniques, 2) arranging external situations to ensure regular writing productivity, 3) facilitating self-control of cognitions and emotions that prevent the recurrence of blocking, and 4) ensuring success in writing via social supports, social skills, and an adaptive sense of audience.

Even as I began the research-based program that would eventually produce a four-step plan, I was learning some basic principles about working with professors as writers. The most far-reaching concerned the nature of solutions for writing problems. As they are typically envisioned, solutions seem deceptively easy: Almost anyone, even the most stymied and cramped writers, can be coaxed into writing something in a first or second attempt. True, getting started may be painful, it may require inspiring people and having them write rapidly about whatever comes to mind, but it occurs quickly, in my experience.

The harder part of helping writers, I discovered, goes far beyond the simple act of establishing momentum. When writers remain productive, they learn to make writing *painless*, *efficient*, and *successful*.

Fortunately, the harder part isn't as difficult as I first supposed. As I revised and refined my writing programs, solutions for these longer-range problems emerged. With but a few exceptions, writers who remained in a schedule requiring an hour or less a weekday of writing mastered a sequence of strategies for remaining truly productive over long periods of time.

How does this occur? The answer, as you might suspect, comprises the rest of this book. It includes the need for changes in both writing habits and attitudes, the need to write regularly, in modest amounts, and the need for success in getting manuscripts appreciated and accepted. For example, most writers benefit in giving up habits of writing such as writing in exhausting binges. Similarly, many writers can learn more adaptive attitudes in writing by not demanding perfection, particularly in rough drafts. Still other professors seem to benefit most from structured exercises that essentially force exposure to new ways of doing or thinking. There is no one best way.

As a writing facilitator, I generally begin with generalizations and analogies. I often remind writers that writing can be as painless and beneficial as good social conversation. Consider the similarities in the two forms of communication: neither is aided by anticipatory nervousness and worry; both come more easily than supposed, once under way; and both offer rewards such as sharing new ideas, sharpening thinking, and establishing a public identity.

Then, depending on the needs of writers, I work toward more specific goals. This manual includes a variety of approaches, experiential and insightful. And, like my earliest programs, the self-help strategies presented here are based in research. This manual represents six years of revising strategies until they worked reliably and endurably with and without my direct presence.[3] While I'm pleased with the development of the unblocking process that seems to work as well with people who never see me as with those who come for weekly sessions, I wonder. Am I engineering myself into obsolescence?

No doubt, I'll remain stubbornly convinced that a personal touch is essential, even when un-measurable. Evidence of that conviction appears here from time to time. In the midst of research-based strategies, I interject the kinds of comments I make in private sessions. I aim to inspire, to calm, to cajole, to counter inevitable doubts . . . and to forgive equally inevitable relapses. I'll especially try to elicit the most critical components of success in writing programs: your willingness to suspend skepticism and a readiness to try things.

All the chapters that follow but the first are prescriptive; they speak directly to recognizing problems and to solving them. The first chapter, in contrast, gives a brief, scholarly overview to the manual. It provides a sense of what the psychology of writing has to say about the usual silence of professors as writers. For readers eager to get on with exercises in solving problems, I recommend skipping or postponing the first chapter.

Notes

[1] An extensive review of the literature on psychological hindrances to writing appears as an annotated bibliography in the appendices at the end of this manual. My initial, pessimistic view of the literature on writing problems changed as I discovered that a) I had been blissfully unaware of some sources and b) the field is growing dramatically.

[2] See, e.g., Boice, R. (1982), Increasing the writing productivity of blocked academicians. *Behaviour Research and Therapy, 20,* 197- 207.

[3] See, e.g., Boice, R. (1983), Experimental and clinical treatments of writing blocks. *Journal of Consulting and Clinical Psychology, 51,* 183-191.

SECTION A:
The Nature of
Writing Problems

Chapter One

Why Professors Don't Write

SCHOLARLY WRITING often seems laborious, slow, and worrisome:[1]

> Telling a writer to relax is like telling a man to relax while being prodded for a hernia . . . He thinks the article must be of a certain length or it won't seem important. He thinks how august it will look in print. He thinks of the people who will read it. He thinks that it must have the solid weight of authority. He thinks that its style must dazzle. No wonder he tightens.

Despite its problems, writing brings more professional rewards than anything else a professor can do. Writing for publication weighs heavily in decisions about hiring, promotion, and tenure in academic and other professional settings.[2] It brings rewards of visibility and portability.[3] And, writing offers a unique kind of self-education:[4]

> I would urge you to write, not because it is a good thing, not because it is nice to see your name in print, not even because it is relevant to full membership in our society, but rather because you will really get to know a field only if you contribute to it . . . Writing ultimately becomes important not only because of what it does for others but also for what it does for oneself.

Why is it then that so few of us write for publication? Of the minority of academicians who write publicly, fewer still account for the bulk of what gets published. Estimates typically attribute some 85% of publications to some 15% of those who could potentially write them.[5]

Academe has traditionally ignored this question. It may be that we subscribe to Social Darwinism, supposing that only the fittest survive. Indeed, those who dominate our journals openly claim that they are among the few who have had the "right stuff" to master the rules of writing for publication. Some of the most successful professors as writers like to say that most other academicians remain silent because they have nothing to say.[6]

Or it may be, given the flood of manuscripts submitted for publication, that professors write too much[7] (although prospects of electronic publishing are removing constraints of pages available in bound journals).[8]

The best answer to the question about why so few of us write may be that we are only beginning to understand the reasons. Academe has been shamefully slow to help its own, especially to make writing for publication easier and more democratic. Because this book aims at remedying those oversights and at beginning with some understanding of writing inhibitions, this chapter focuses on what is known about writing problems.

Causes of Writing Problems

Most knowledge about writing problems is conjectural. Most is limited to single factors such as perfectionism or procrastination. But, the psychology of writing is becoming more empirically-based, and we can gain valuable insights about what inhibits writers by surveying its literature. This chapter organizes that literature into six main subject headings, beginning with the most commonly attributed causes of writing problems.

Censors

Freud[9] was one of many who helped make this cause of writing problems well-known. He borrowed an idea from the dramatist Schiller in using the notion of internal censors to explain what keeps writers from writing: Our "watchers at the gates" critically examine ideas as they vie for conscious consideration; when left to their own devices, the watchers reject too soon and discriminate too severely. The result can be premature editing that keeps us from getting ideas on paper unless they seem safe and perfect.

Nowadays we typically replace the label of internal censors with internal critics. Same thing. And, more often than in Freud's day, we go on to speculate about the sources of these inner voices.[10]

When you can hear him, the internal critic speaks in a shrill, querulous tone, rational, dour, often pessimistic, alert only to the dangers of the world around us and therefore to the shortcomings in our work. Assuming the voices of parents, teachers, and other authority figures, he whispers and sometimes shouts that our writing is bad. His often snide voice judges the quality and correctness of our prose. . . . He edits words and thoughts before we have a chance to put them on paper, and thus creates blank-page panic. He rejects angles, intuitions, and conceptual frameworks before we have even a remote chance to explore our alternatives.

The consensus about internal critics is this: They do more than induce bad feelings about our own writing. They even undermine our ability to generate ideas, creativity, and confidence.[11]

Fears of Failure

Fears of failure as a cause of writing inhibitions are listed commonly and in a variety of related forms: a) negative self-attitudes,[12] b) negative self-statements,[13] c) phobias,[14] and d) self-fulfilling prophecies.[15] While psychologists have garnered a lot of information about test anxiety, social phobias, and other activities (such as sexual functioning) that require unself-conscious performance, they still know little about fears of failure in writing.

The best information about fears of writing comes from communications researchers. Daly's[16] pioneering work on writing apprehension includes a standardized assessment device based on 63 items about writing in dimensions such as recollections of having one's writing judged by others. Correlational studies based on Daly's assessments provide some insights about the nature of writing apprehension. Some are obvious; e.g., "high apprehensives" tend to shy away from careers or positions that demand much writing. Some results may not be obvious; e.g., high apprehensives allow themselves too little time for the planning and prefiguring of prewriting, for editing a finished draft, and even for the overall completion of a manuscript.

Daly's research also reveals an interesting breadth to writing apprehension. What initially looked like little more than fears of evaluation (and, at worst, of public exposure as a failure and fraud) now is known to include related problems procrastination, maladaptive writing habits, rigid beliefs about how to write, etc.

Perfectionism

Traditionally, perfectionism stands as a major and separate cause of writing problems. No wonder. All of us, at one time or another, have experienced the urge to keep reworking material until it seems perfect. All of us, at some level, would like to be seen as excellent writers.

Some writers let perfectionism thoroughly block them; their ideas and papers never do reach acceptable levels of perfection, they can never do enough revising or rechecking, they even develop obsessive concerns with detail.[17] At their worst, perfectionists are not only unproductive as writers. They are also elitists and snobs who assume that most published writing lacks merit or quality and that their writing, should they decide to finish and share it, would rise above the commonplace.

In a way, perfectionism overlaps with fears of failure. Perfectionism practiced pathologically, as a morbid fear of making mistakes and of being exposed as mediocre, is little more than a fear of failure that inhibits writing.

Procrastination

Writing, because it is usually practiced as a "non-recurring task" and without short-term rewards, lends itself to procrastination.[18] Moreover, we often set up weak, ineffective programs to ensure regular progress and to preclude distractions. And we procrastinate because we are reluctant to impose on others in getting tasks done in timely fashion and too ready to wait for others to take the initiative.[19]

We can even, with some justification, blame tendencies to procrastination on cultural pressures to compete and definitions of success in terms of impossibly high standards. In this view, procrastination assumes some adaptiveness as an understandable mechanism for coping with aversive pressures:[20]

> In a setting where teachers seem to have all the authority, procrastination is one way you, the student, could exert some control of your own by not following the rules or by turning work in late or not at all.

Perhaps the best explanations of procrastination combine both the outer and inner factors. Albert Ellis, the famous psychotherapist, provides one such combination.[21] He distinguishes kinds of procrastination (e.g., in reaching self-development goals, in inconveniencing others). He assumes that the delays in procrastination come from foolish, needless choices that inconvenience ourselves and others. And, Ellis supposes that three personality characteristics predispose people to procrastinate: self-doubting that causes delays and then self-condemning that follows the procrastination; low frustration tolerance that leads to giving up easily; and a passive-aggressive style of frustrating the people who are kept waiting.

Another systematic view of procrastination comes from questionnaire research with students. One group of procrastinators distinguished itself by responding strongly to items about fear of failure (evaluation anxiety, perfectionism, and low self-confidence). The second showed procrastination more clearly tied to the aversiveness of the task being put off; these students tended to show low levels of energy, planfulness, and decisiveness.[22]

Early Experience

While early experiences in writing, usually of a negative variety, seem to be part of all the causes of problems listed here, this category typically merits consideration of its own. Primary-level teachers get the brunt of the blame. They are recalled for undermining students' confidence as writers,[12] for excluding playfulness from writing,[23] and for providing little useful knowledge about ways of improving writing.[24] Teachers do seem to foster unproductive myths about writing, especially the belief that good writing cannot be taught (and must, therefore, be learned by trial and error).[25]

Mental Health

Tradition holds that writing, especially creative writing, depends on psychopathology. It also assumes the reverse, that poor mental health stymies writers.

Much of the association between writing and psychopathology comes from writers who revel in presenting themselves as asocial, suspicious, gloomy, and quarrelsome.[26] But these damning self-portrayals prove very little. It may be that writers differ from non-writers in mental health only in terms of their readiness to admit their foibles publicly.

Still, assumptions about the unhealthiness of writing comprise a popular area of reflection about writers and their writing problems. Most commonly, scholars look for correlations between success in writing and mood disorders (usually depression, mania, and even suicidality). Manic depressiveness seems salient among writers, especially poets (e.g., Lowell, Jarrell, and Roethke). In one such study of 47 British artists and writers, 38% sought treatment for mood disorders, a rate much higher than that attributed to the general population.[27] In another study, 50 writers at a prominent university workshop were followed for 15 years. Some 80% of these writers, compared to 30% of a control group, showed mood disorders; some 30%, compared to 7%, had problems with alcohol consumption.[27]

The conclusion from such studies: Creativity in writing depends on moderate ("subclinical") levels of mood disorder. What is a virtue in moderation becomes a liability in excess as the moods that once brought energy and sharpened perceptions turn to uncontrollable irritation and hopelessness.[28] The answer, then, to sorting out the relationship between mood and writing seems to lie in moderation. Writing, like other activities requiring intense concentration, induces tension, irritability, and even obsessiveness. Practiced in binges it invites mood disorders.[29] Practiced in brief, daily sessions it brings consistent productivity and satisfaction.[30]

Personality Types

Tradition, again, holds strong views about relationships between writing and personality types. As with psychopathology, popular beliefs form a dim view of writers. So, for example, scientific writers are portrayed as unsociable, skeptical, overachieving, and masculine.[31] Teachers, in contrast, are depicted as sociable, emotionally stable, liberal, and esthetically sensitive.[32] The upshot of such studies is confirmation of professors' beliefs that writing must come at the expense of social skills and teaching commitment. In fact, the few studies that afford faculty incentives to excel in all three dimensions writing, collegiality, and teaching show those activities to be mutually facilitative.[33]

One of the unusually practical examinations of writers' personalities helps us sort out their styles of productivity.[34] The majority of researchers/writers (75%) are classified as silent. Writers judged as mass-producers or prolific writers tended to be men; mass-producers tend to be highly competitive and energetic but, curiously, abandon writing in the face of indifferent receptions by colleagues. Women, in this scheme, typically fit descriptions as silent or perfectionistic writers.[35]

Traditional assumptions about women and writing are changing, incidentally. Realities, especially facts about the equivalency of younger men and women as writers and publishers, have forced these changes in view; we will revisit such considerations anon.

Working Habits and Attitudes

Another change in traditional thinking is shown in this and in subsequent causes of working problems. We increasingly recognize that writers' personalities as, say, perfectionists, carry only part of the blame for low levels of productivity, satisfaction, and success in writing. So too for early experiences including poor writing teachers. We now know that the habits and conditions under which writers work can be at least as problematic. Because this manual aims at helping professors change both their personal styles and conditions for writing, the remaining considerations in Chapter 1 are critical to understanding this approach.

Consider some of what we know about professors' writing habits from recent surveys. Many professors write in ways they know are less than optimal. They tend to save writing for times when they are tired, having spent fresher hours of the day on less valued tasks. Still, those who write most fluently and successfully provide clues about effective habits: these professors as writers follow fairly regular schedules of writing, avoid bingeing in writing, feel less anxiety about writing, and express little resentment toward the editorial process.[36] Not surprisingly, this group shows an increasing reliance on word processors.[37]

There are also signs, as suggested earlier, of changing involvement by academic women as writers and publishers. Olsen's book, *Silences*, is the best-known accounting of distractions and discouragements to women who wanted to write.[38] She calculated that, for most of our literate history, men outnumbered women as writers by 12 to 1. With changing policies of hiring, supporting, even scholarly reviewing of women in academe, we can expect improvements in that ratio. Recent surveys confirm that expectation. In one study of 300 university psychologists, male respondents had published a mean of 7.8 articles in the last three years compared to 7.3 articles for a similar group of women. Newer Ph.D.s showed even closer productivity rates.[39]

Still, a sign of inequity persists. Women, more often than men (47% vs. 27%), felt excessive pressures to publish amidst busy schedules. Women, more often than men (87% vs. 74%), were unable to ignore rude editorial rejections. And women (27% vs. 4%) more often imagined that women get harsher treatment than do men in the editorial process.[39] So, while old assumptions that women wouldn't work as hard or as doggedly at scholarly writing have been disproven, another doubt has risen in its place. Where women match men's levels of writing productivity, will they do so happily? One guess is that they will, once accustomed and once treated with complete equanimity. Another guess is that women will help change academic pressures for publication to be less competitive and rejecting ordeals.

Work Habits and Busyness

The single most commonly listed reason for not writing by academicians is a lack of time. Most professors who don't write put the blame on busyness. Accordingly, traditional surveys of professors show them to be very busy, with estimates of typical workweeks at 60-80 hours.[30]

Direct observational studies of professors at work suggest an important difference from studies based around professors' self-reports. Almost all of us, even professors with heavy teaching loads, have several 20-30 minute blocks of time available for writing in most workweeks. Because we tend to suppose that writing must be done in large blocks of time, we fail to see busy weeks during semesters as appropriate for writing productivity.

In fact, though, professors who try doing writing in brief, daily sessions during busy weeks evidence two benefits. First, they typically produce far more writing than do colleagues who work in binges, and they do so at rates more than sufficient to meet the expectations of tenure/promotion committees on campus. Second, they find writing more enjoyable–in part because it no longer requires substantial warm-up times and in part because they no longer need to take it home to complete it.

An Integrated Look at Causes of Writing Problems

Overall, we now know that most writing problems of professors fall into two main categories. One we just reviewed: Professors who wait until they are fully ready and undistracted tend to do very little writing. The second deals with the personal styles of writers visited earlier.

New studies of productive and unproductive writers provide specific and useful information about the changes in personal styles necessary to achieve more efficient, effective writing. One study distinguished writers as professors into the four categories shown here:[37]

Four Types of Already Productive Academic Writers

	Enthusiastic	*Anxious*
Thinkers	30%	24%
Doers	38%	8%

Doers, predictably, do better, in terms of productivity, than thinkers. Anxiety, much like self-conscious thinking, doesn't seem to help writers. Anxious doers, incidentally, were nearly nonexistent, perhaps because doers tend to compose enthusiastically and spontaneously.

Another recent study of professors as writers used the assessment of writing problems that appears at the end of this manual.[40] It puts typologies of writers in terms of personal styles we saw earlier in this chapter–of perfectionism, procrastination, etc. An additional type also emerged, of aversion to the fatigue and demands of writing; we saw a suggestion of such a factor in our consideration of procrastinators.

In a sample of 100 faculty participating in programs to enhance their writing, the following patterns of writing problems emerged as most typical:

Most Frequent Clusters of Diagnostic Patterns on the Blocking Questionnaire

1. Work apprehension and low energy re writing
2. Dysphoria and evaluation anxiety
3. Perfectionism
4. Procrastination and impatience

Two things stand out in these common patterns of writing problems among professors seeking help with writing: First, except for the instance of perfectionism, common writing problems include a combination of two components. Second, the combinations that distinguish problem writers make sense in terms of what we saw earlier. Procrastination works (or inhibits) hand-in-hand with impatience. Depression, especially its obsessive and worrisome aspects, has links to fears of evaluation. And, a general aversion to the demands and fatigue of writing is akin to a higher than normal level of self-perceived laziness about writing.

What We Can Learn From Analyzing Writing Problems

In my experience, professors contemplating changes in their habits and attitudes derive several benefits in taking a brief look at the nature of writing problems. Doing so reminds us what a fascinating topic writing is; most professors simply enjoy thinking and talking about the subject. Once reminded of this fascination, many of us approach the prospect of writing with a bit more enthusiasm and curiosity.

Curiosity helps bring focus to writing problems. What ordinarily gets described in terms of vague labels like blocking has, as we just saw, a variety of specific problem patterns, each of which demands separate consideration. In other words, we gain in beginning a writing program by having identified the specifics of our writing problems and by having established some awareness of their nature.

Doing so does more than establish focus; it also establishes an important sense of generality. By seeing the variety of writing problems and by recognizing their commonality among professors, we get past the limiting impression that our writing problems are unique.

A final caution remains, however. Having started with a greater sense of comfort and readiness for managing writing, we should resist a common temptation of putting aside the prescriptive exercises that follow. In fact, insights about writing problems do not translate readily into lasting changes in attitudes and habits. The key ingredient in effecting that translation is the tested series of experiential tasks that follow.

So it is that from here on out I abandon the familiar, third-person style of scholarly writing of Chapter 1. In the chapters that follow I talk more directly, aiming to take you through a series of self-help programs for professors as writers. I hope that you'll combine the two experiences, this scholarly overview and the prescriptive exercises, in ways that tally how well expectations—yours and mine—are met.

Notes

[1] Zinsser, W. (1980). *On writing well*. New York: Harper and Row.

[2] Bayer, A. E., & Astin, H. S. (1975). Sex differentials in the academic reward system. *Science, 88,* 796-802.

[3] Mahoney, M. J. (1979). Psychology of the scientist. *Social Studies of Science, 9,* 349-375.

[4] Orne, M. T. (1981). The why and how of a communication to the literature. *International Journal of Clinical and Experimental Hypnosis, 29,* 1-4.

[5] Cole, J. R. (1981). Women in science. *American Scientist, 69,* 385-391

[6] Boice, R. (1987). *How to write like an academician*. Manuscript submitted for publication.

[7] Quaytman, W. (1968, Winter). Psychotherapist's writing block. V*oices, 14,* 13-17.

[8] Brand, S. (1987). *The Media Lab: Inventing the future at MIT.* New York: Viking.
Hiltz, S. R. (1978). Impact of a computerized conferencing system upon scientific research specialties. *Journal of Research Communication Studies, 1,* 117-124.

[9] Freud, S. (1900). *The interpretation of dreams.* (A. A. Brill, Trans., 1913). New York: Macmillan.

[10] Mack, K., & Skjei, E. (1979). *Overcoming writing blocks.* Los Angeles: J. P. Tarcher.

[11] Harris, M. (1985). Diagnosing writing-process problems: A pedagogical application of speaking-aloud protocol analysis. In M. Rose (Ed.), *When a writer can't write* (pp. 166-181). New York: Guilford Press.

[12] Kronsky, B. J. (1979). Freeing the creative process: The relevance of Gestalt. *Art Psychotherapy, 6,* 233-240.

[13] Boice, R. (1985). Cognitive components of blocking. *Written Communication, 2,* 91-104.

[14] Himadi, W. G, Boice, R., & Barlow, D. H. (1985). Assessment of agoraphobia. *Behaviour Research & Therapy, 23,* 311-323.

[15]Boice, R., & Jones, F. (1984). Why academicians don't write. *Journal of Higher Education, 55*, 567-582.

[16]Daly, J. A. (1985). Writing apprehension. In M. Rose (Ed.), *When a writer can't write*. New York: Guilford Press.

[17]Goodman, P. (1952). On writer's block. *Complex, 7*, 42-50.

[18]Dillon, M. J., Kent, H. M., & Malott, R. W. (1980). A supervisory system for accomplishing long-range projects: An application to master's thesis research. *Journal of Organizational Behavior Management, 2*, 213-227.

[19]Lakein, A. (1973). *How to get control of your time and your life*. New York: Signet.

[20]Burka, J. B., & Yuen, L. M. (1983). *Procrastination: Why you do it, what to do about it*. Reading, MA: Addison-Wesley.

[21]Ellis, A., & Knaus, W. J. (1977). *Overcoming procrastination*. New York: Institute for Rational Living.

[22]Solomon, L. J., & Rothblum, E. D. (1984). Academic procrastination: Frequency and cognitive-behavioral correlates. *Journal of Counseling Psychology, 31*, 503-509.

[23]Emig, J. (1981). Non-magical thinking. In C. H. Frederiksen & J. F. Dominic (Eds.), *Writing: Process, development, and communication*. Hillsdale, NJ: Erlbaum.

[24]Flower, L. S., & Hayes, J. R. (1977). Problem-solving strategies and the writing process. *College English, 39*, 449- 461.

[25]Stack, R. (1980). Writing as conversation. *Visible Language, 14*, 376-382.

[26]Ellenberger, H. F. (1970). *The discovery of the unconscious*. New York: Basic Books.

[27]Holden, C. (1987, April). Creativity and the troubled mind. *Psychology Today*, pp. 9-10.

[28]Holkeboer, R. (1986). *Creative agony: Why writers suffer*. Briston, IN: Wyndham Hall Press.

[29]Boice, R. (1988). *Psychology of writing*. Manuscript submitted for publication.

[30]Boice, R. (1987). Is released time an effective component of faculty development programs? *Research in Higher Education, 26*, 311-326.

[31]Terman, L. M. (1955, January). Are scientists different? *Scientific American*, No. 437.

Cattell, R. B. (1962). The personality and motivation of the researcher from measurements of contemporaries and from biography. In C. W. Taylor and F. Barron (Eds.), *Scientific creativity: Its recognition and development*. New York: Wiley.

McClelland, D. C. (1962). The calculated risk: An aspect of scientific performance. In C. W. Taylor & F. Barron (Eds.), *Scientific creativity: Its recognition and development*. New York: Wiley.

Helmreich, R. L., Spence, J. T., Beane, W. E., Lucker, G. W., & Matthews, K. A. (1980). Making it in academic psychology: Demographic and personality correlates of attainment. *Journal of Personality and Social Psychology, 39*, 896-908.

[32]Costin, G., & Grush, J. E. (1973). Personality correlates of teacher-student behavior in the college classroom. *Journal of Educational Psychology, 65*, 35-44.

Rushton, P., Murray, H. G., & Paunonen, S. V. (1983). Personality, research creativity, and teaching effectiveness in universities. *Scientometrics, 5*, 93-116.

[33]Boice, R. (1984). Reexamination of traditional emphases in faculty development. *Research in Higher Education, 21*, 195- 209.

[34]Cole, J. R., & Cole, S. (1973). *Social stratification in science.* Chicago: University of Chicago Press.

[35]Over, R. (1982). Research productivity and impact of male and female psychologists. *American Psychologist. 37*, 24-31.

[36]Boice, R., & Johnson, K. (1984). Perceptions of writing and publication amongst faculty at a doctoral degree granting university. *Research in Higher Education, 21*, 33-43.

[37]Hartley, J., & Branthwaite, A. (1987). The psychologist as wordsmith: A question-naire study of the writing strategies of productive British psychologists. Manu-script submitted for publication.

[38]Olsen, T. (1979). One out of twelve: Women who are writers in our century. In S. Ruddick & P. Daniels (Eds.), *Working it out.* New York: Pantheon.

[39]Boice, R., Shaughnessy, P., & Pecker, G. (1985). Women and publishing in psychol-ogy. *American Psychologist, 40*, 577 578.

[40]Boice, R., & Turner, J. L. (1987, April). *A longitudinal study of faculty careers.* Paper presented at Western Psychological Association Convention, Long Beach, CA.

Chapter Two

The Phenomenology of Writing Problems

I USUALLY BEGIN first meetings by asking colleagues for experiential accounts of their recent efforts to write. Then, after we've talked about their experiences and problems, we read a sampling of phenomenological accounts of other problem writers. One of my favorites is this dramatic, public self-disclosure by Virginia Valian:[1]

> I worked steadily, though with difficulty and anxiety; I knew, however, that I could last out five minutes of difficulty and anxiety, so I continued. At last the bell went off and I collapsed. I went into the bedroom and threw myself on the bed, breathing hard and feeling my heart race.

Valian's account of an initial attempt to write typically elicits two reactions: First, writers express relief that someone else has had so much difficulty with writing. Then, they wonder why I used an example of someone who had already managed to start writing.

I respond with my first of many reminders that productive writing is much more than getting unstuck. And I elaborate with histories of writers who failed to move beyond the pain and inefficiency characterized by Valian: they either restuck or else did much less writing than they hoped to.

Sharing writing experiences helps combat the privateness and mysteriousness on which blocks thrive. Problem writers benefit in learning that their own experiences are not so unique as they imagined. Colleagues benefit in becoming better observers of writing problems in themselves and in others.[2] And, as they learn more about writing, writers build the confidence to face writing problems as understandable, manageable problems.

One way to develop a sense of comfort with the topic is to peruse the literature on writing problems. That's no small task; you might like to put it off. Most of the literature appears in the summaries collected at the end of this book. I advise you to do it only when you're in the mood–advice I do not give about writing.

Another, more immediately useful way to establish familiarity with writing problems extends what we've already been doing–reading brief accounts of other people's blocking experiences.

When I'm with a writer, I proceed through categories just as I'll do here, moving from common to fairly uncommon types.

Anecdotal Accounts

Distaste for Writing

By far the most salient of all but a few recollections by problem writers of attempts to write is a dislike for writing. They talk about how hard, fatiguing, and demanding it seems, as in these transcribed accounts from three writers:

- "You probably won't like this. I hate to write. At least I do now. I'd rather clean the house. [laughs] I'd rather do almost anything else. I mean writing is a strain. I remember straining to figure out *what* to say. And then *how* to say it. It's much easier to talk about my ideas. That's much easier."
- "Even before I tried to begin I was already thinking about how exhausted I'd be. How tired I'd be after flailing away for a few hours. Do you know what I mean? And I was tired, even though I wrote for only about an hour." [question: "Was it a pleasant kind of exhaustion?"] "No, I really didn't like it. It shouldn't be so exhausting."
- [laughs] "I'd rather not think about it because whenever I do, I think about how difficult it is for me. Writing does *not* come easily for me, if it comes at all. When it comes, it happens slowly, painfully. I write about as fast as a snail. [laughs] And about as well."

Later, once involved in writing programs, each of these writers volunteered comments about how much easier writing had become. But they hadn't forgotten how distasteful and difficult writing once was.

Lack of Time for Writing

Initial reflections on recent writing experiences also include nearly universal concerns about feeling rushed and too busy:

- "I actually spent more time worrying about not having enough time to write and about how I'll never get caught up on my writing than I did writing. Does that make sense? No, but that's how I felt. I felt rushed and annoyed. Annoyed that I had too many other things to do. Rushed because I didn't have enough time to do it right."
- "What I did was to use the best reason for me not to write. Not enough time. I told myself that I didn't have enough time and it was the truth." [question: "What happened then?"] "I decided to do something else, something more pressing, I think." [laughs]

Here again, complaints eventually diminished as the writers persisted in their unblocking programs. Two techniques, as we'll see later, probably helped: learning to write in brief, free periods during weekdays, and other management techniques. In case you're wondering, I've yet to meet any professor who couldn't make time for regular writing that accumulated into meaningful manuscripts. I expect you to begin with a bit of skepticism.

Lack of Confidence

This category completes the experiential accounts of blocking that approach universality—with some stretching of the ground rules. Ready admission of confidence problems doesn't always come quickly, especially for males. But, sooner or later, almost all the writers with whom I have worked recalled recent times when a lack of confidence interfered with writing. These are samples from first sessions only:

- "I felt timid when I was writing. I found that I was *surprising* myself with what I was writing, or at least with the boldness of what I thought of writing." [question: "So you didn't write some of the things you wanted to?"] "I didn't feel ready to be so decisive. I started thinking of who I am, a nobody really."
- "I just thought about writing and I realized that I have yet to build a body of knowledge, a major contribution. I'm not ready. I certainly wasn't ready then. In the past, my efforts have often led down dark, blind dead ends. Perhaps it's nonsense to believe that I can contribute."

- "Here's what I was thinking. I'm good at finding data to support my conclusions. Only I'm scared that the conclusions are wrong."
- "There are often two parts of me. The bright, knowledgeable person who can talk intelligently. Then the person who feels as if she has no expertise. That was the central issue. The extent to which I trust my own knowledge."
- "I thought of a colleague, a woman, who is much brighter than I am. She's had all the right connections, family, education at the right places. I'm afraid of her." [question: "Afraid of what?"] "Of being found out. [laughs] That I'm really not very intelligent."
- "I was worried about having stolen other people's ideas. I was thinking that _____'s article was very similar to what I'm doing. That I was just rehashing it. Yet upon rereading, I find little similarity. I wonder why I have difficulty taking credit for originality. Yet, everything I do seem to come from elsewhere, other people. Yet, that is absurd. I am bright. I am clever. I'm very aware of that in my personal interactions. Why not in my professional?"

Writers generally enjoy listening to anecdotes about low self-confidence in other writers. As they relate these stories, I try to make a basic point: I ask writers to recall how clearly and directly and interestingly the other writers spoke. In fact, I note, even problem writers have something captivating and worthwhile to say.

But, demonstration doesn't always lead to immediate changes in cognitions and behaviors. Consider what happened when I restated what one writer had said in her *own* experiential account and emphasized how interesting and well-stated it was. She said: "Oh. [laughs] No. No. I could agree with that for the topic but not for the writer."

Writing Anxiety

About half of writers with whom I have worked emphasized anxiety in their recollections of writing attempts. Curiously, some 60% of those were actually recalling things that hadn't been incapacitating since school days. Whether recent or not, memories of strong writing anxiety remained real and frightening. The examples here represent a continuum of experiences, with a mild form followed by a strong form:

- "I got nervous. I even started to shake a bit, kind of like stage fright, you know. I get really nervous before speeches at conventions. And I wish I could do something about it, but I just suffer through it." [question: "Were you able to just suffer through the writing despite your shakiness?"] "No, that's just it. I can't really get out of speaking once I'm there, but I can put off the writing. And that's what I did."

- "Well, I tried to write this morning, because I knew I'd be coming here. [laughs] I fell apart. [long pause] Just like I usually do. I could hardly catch my breath. I worried about whether I would pass out. I just couldn't sit there, so I got up and took a walk. Other times I can do it. I can write. But not today."
- "I had what my physician calls a panic attack. I take medication when I know I'm going to be in a frightening situation. I did then, but it didn't help much. I felt like I was having a heart attack. The first thing I did when I felt my heart pounding was to reassure myself that I would *not* try to write. That's why I haven't written anything for [pause] years."

Inability to Start Writing

People who can't start writing offer some of the most memorable accounts of writing problems. I recall three writers whose recent attempts at writing resulted in all-night efforts to write a perfect first sentence or paragraph. One simply waved the blank page at me when I asked for an experiential account. For him, that said enough. The other, less annoyed, non-starters gave these descriptions:

- "I can tell you exactly what happened. I was thinking of what a great paper I would write. I got into thinking about the kind of paper my advisor in grad school would write, a really good paper. So I knew what I wanted to do, but I wasn't sure how I would say it. I mostly sat and stared at a few sentences that I didn't like."
- "I kept stopping to revise. When I revised, I started over. And eventually I came to a standstill. I was sick of what I was writing and I couldn't do any better with new starts."

Inability to Finish Writing

Problem writing as an inability to finish resembles its counterpart, an inability to start, in dynamics such as perfectionism. But, despite their similarities, the two forms of writing problems typically occur in different people.

Once started, in my experience, writers with initial difficulties are impatient to finish. Non-finishers, on the other hand, don't struggle much over beginnings; they know that perfection comes later, in multiple revisions. Some non-finishers even write prolifically, without ever completing their projects.

When revisions prove endless and frustrating, non-finishers seek help, often reluctantly. Their complaints may be vague:

- [question: "How may I help?"] "By helping me find ways to make writing more efficient. I waste too much time."

In this case, a non-finisher demonstrated a typical problem. He did not seem to recognize his specific problem. Subsequent questioning in the first session often led to uncoverings like this one:

- [question: "Let's see if I understand; you don't have problems working at writing?"] "No. I keep working at it." [question: "So what might keep you from feeling you're doing a good job?"] "It doesn't get anywhere. [pause] No, that's not really true. Each time I think I'm finished, I see that there's a lot more to do. I always see ways to improve the writing. I worry about its going off for review with some terrible flaw in it." [question: "What kind of flaw?"] "A critical reference missing or an analysis that was done wrong . . ." [later question: "Now, if you'll imagine that we've done thorough checks for flaws via colleagues' reviews of your rough draft, then would you feel ready to say it's finished?"] "Well, I don't know. I'd still like to play around with the wording a bit more. It's easy to do now that I'm working on the word processor . . ." [question: "How would you know when it's good enough?"] "It's really good enough now. [laughs] I'm just thinking. I did the same thing on my dissertation. Over a year in revisions. My advisor finally forced me to stop."

Other Psychological Disruptors

Depression. Emotional turmoil, as we all know, can disrupt writing. Chronic turmoil, particularly when it settles into depression, helps ensure lasting disruptions. Indeed, depression and blocking resemble each other in symptoms (e.g., passivity giving up) and remedies (e.g., action getting back to adaptive activities despite their seeming aversiveness). While I'm never sure which came first, the writing problem or the depression, I'm not surprised when these problem writers have little to say about the phenomenology of blocking:

- "What happened? I just sat there. [pause] I looked out the window, mostly. I couldn't bring myself to write."

Why are depressed people so non-expressive? Because, evidently, severe depression reduces energy and increases negativity, including a sense of helplessness in even talking about it. To the extent that blocking is a lack of momentum, depression in problem writers creates obvious problems. Fortunately for depressed writers, lack of momentum is typically no more difficult to counter than perfectionism and other disruptive factors.

Phobias. Consider emotional turmoil at another level, where the writing itself seems to be the source of discomfort. That discomfort in some people produces such thoroughgoing avoidance that their response to writing becomes phobic.

Closer examination of phobic writers reveals something surprising about their efforts to avoid writing. These colleagues work hardest at avoiding the anticipation of writing and the uncomfortable anxiety it provokes. That is, they are fearful of fear. As a rule, this situation perpetuates blocking because it keeps its victims from retesting beliefs that attempts to write are tantamount to disaster.

Sometimes, phobic writers avoid help and manage to build professional careers that minimize the need to write.[3] Those who actually seek help arrive, understandably, in discomfort. They say little about the experience of trying to write at first; later, they may report recollections of panic attacks during writing. Mainly, phobic writers emphasize the relief felt in getting out of writing tasks:

- "When I realized that a term paper would be required, I switched enrollment to audit the course. I knew there was no way I'd write a paper." [question: "What would you do if you got into a situation where you *had* to write a paper like that one?"] "I don't even want to think about it."

As far as I can tell, many phobic writers manage life as reasonably as do phobics who avoid elevators or airplanes. Sometimes, however, lifestyles require facing up to these feared activities, even to seeking help. Then, if the writers are brave enough, cures, full or partial, are usually managed.

One message in this preview of psychological disruptions is that we, however unwittingly, tend to be our own most powerful agents of writing problems.

Writing cramps,[4] the final example of a problem style in this chapter, provides a reminder of self-destructive tendencies. In mild form, one familiar to most of us, some part of our writing arm cramps up during writing. I recall a freshman essay exam where my wrist became so stiff I could hardly finish. In serious form, writing cramps prevent writers from producing more than a scribble.

Experiential accounts of cramping rarely go beyond the physical pains:

- "I could feel my hand and wrist stiffening up as I got ready to write. By the time I tried to begin, I could hardly hold the pencil. I couldn't go on."

If you've had severe cramps, you can imagine how effectively they block writing. Perhaps you can also sympathize with cramped writers who are reluctant to suppose that their cramps are self-engendered ways to avoid writing.

In a sense, though, that's where we all must begin. Solutions proceed more quickly when we admit our own undermining strategies of disrupting writing. Even most disruptions that begin in our environments (e.g., time pressures, discouraging work conditions) can hinder us chronically only if we choose to let them.

Preliminary Self-Diagnosis and Conclusions

Why, once again, take time for self-study with writers eager to get on with writing? Because, for one thing, impatience is a powerful ally of writing problems. And, because not all problem styles require the same correctives. Writing cramps, for instance, require specialized techniques of muscle relaxation and even hypnosis to ensure relatively painless momentum.[5]

By learning more about our styles of writing, we arm ourselves against another powerful ally of problems, relapses. In my experience, even the most enthusiastic and conscientious participants eventually face conditions where they fall back into old problem patterns. Careful observation of our writing habits and attitudes means an increased likelihood of recognizing the early forms of symptoms creeping back in.

It is, of course, one thing to read about self-disclosure and self-observation, and another to do it. So, I'd like you to approximate what

I have writers do in their first meeting with me. Please think back to your most recent attempts to write. Simply talk the experience out loud. Then, enter it here–without editing or without concern about how polished it sounds. This record can provide an invaluable reminder later on when you're writing productively, successfully, and comfortably, when you may have forgotten some of the problem experiences.

Describe your most recent attempts to write, especially those with problems.

Notes

[1]Valian, V. (1977, Learning to work. In S. Ruddick & P. Daniels (Eds.), *Working it out.* New York: Pantheon.

[2]Observation as an aid to behavior change is reviewed in Boice, R. (1983), Observational skills, *Psychological Bulletin, 93,* 3- 29, and in a delightfully useful analogy of how seeing can be translated into writing by Edwards, B. (1979), *Drawing on the right side of the brain.* Los Angeles: J. P. Tarcher.

[3]John Daly, the pioneer in research on writing apprehension, describes the lengths to which some people go to avoid writing (e.g., writing apprehension). In M. Rose (Ed.), *When a writer can't write.* New York: Guilford, 1985.

[4]Writing cramps occasion a surprisingly broad literature, some very old, most published in Europe. See, e.g., Sanavio, L. (1979), A wider model of writer's cramp. *Behavior Analysis and Modification, 4,* 17-27.

[5]See, for an example of automatic writing techniques that help uncramp writers, Boice, R. (1985), Psychotherapies for writing blocks. In M. Rose Ed.), *When a writer can't write.* New York: Guilford.

Chapter Three

Assessment of Writing Problems

IF YOU WERE CONSULTING me directly for help with blocking, this would be our second meeting. In all likelihood, your initial comments would include something like this actual sample:

- "You know, after I left, I realized you didn't say much about getting me started. I liked your description of a program that helps make writing efficient and painless, although I wonder if that would happen to me. When do we get going?"

You'd be right. I don't always rush people into getting started. The closest I come to pressuring writing is an offhand comment at the end of the first session. I ask clients to begin keeping a chart to bring to all writing sessions. I ask you to do the same thing. (A copy of the format appears on the page 31 as Figure 2. It can be photocopied for use unless you prefer real graph paper or some other medium.)

The graph represents a critical habit in mastering writing. It makes us aware of the prospect of writing on a daily basis, whether we write or not. So, it's important to prepare a graph and to begin making entries, even before you're writing. Sometimes the chart alone, especially the guilt of posting up a wasted day, is stimulus enough to get people writing.

A chart for people who begin on their own usually looks like the one shown in Figure 1.

As people do begin (and again, there's no hurry for the moment), they invariably have questions. They ask about how to count pages for the chart:

"What if I write on legal pads, in big, sloppy handwriting?"

"What if I'm only making revisions on something that's already written?"

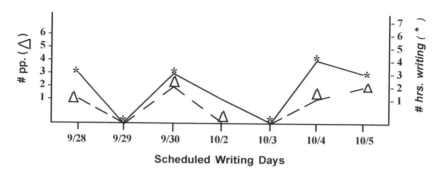

Figure 1: Writing Progress of Writers

The answers are simple. Most professors, in fact know how to convert their handwritten pages into typed-equivalent pages. In cases where something like note taking or revisions doesn't translate easily to typed-equivalent pages, I ask for best estimates. The point isn't so much accuracy as maintaining a record of the output related to writing. Where you think the entry is questionable, make a note of what you were doing on the graph.

But what, you may still ask, about the original question of when we get going?

I respond with another caution about impatience. I talk briefly about making real beginnings next session (or chapter). I express my sympathy for people who've waited to seek help until they feel pressures to produce writing immediately. And I survey prospects for turning out lots of writing in the next few months:

- "If you stick with this, you'll soon be in a regimen where you write four to five days a week, maybe for 30 minutes or an hour a day. Most people, once under way, can write from one to three pages each session. So, even with an eye to sensible quality and necessary revision, that usually means at least 100-150 usable manuscript pages in the next six months. Unless you're Isaac Asimov, that's a lot of writing."

Then I add another point. We *are* already going. What we're doing now is critical to dealing effectively with almost all writing problems. Slowing down for initial self-assessments is much like what com-

of typed-page equivalents

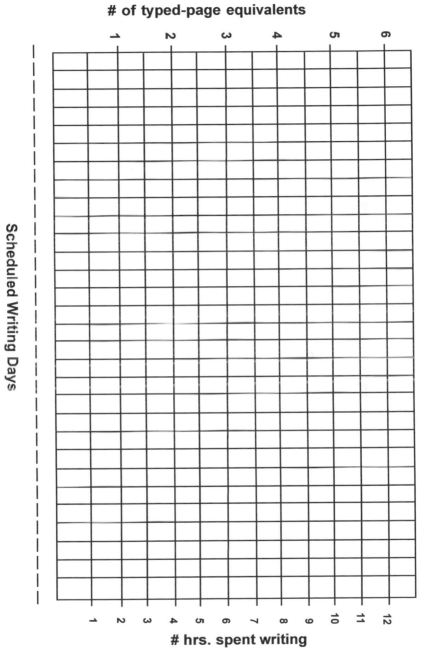

Scheduled Writing Days

 # hrs. spent writing

Figure 2: Writing Progress Chart

position teachers call prewriting. Prewriting includes building knowledge about writing and preparing conceptual materials, a procedure that can speed and improve writing projects in the long run. In my experience, problem writers usually dislike prewriting, perhaps because writing problems and impatience are so often interrelated.

For the moment, then, it makes sense to learn a bit more about ourselves as writers.

Self-Assessments of Blocking

Chapter 2 provided a sense of general problem styles and informal notions of what happens to other writers with writing problems. In this chapter I ask you to extend self-analysis to formal assessments. Whether or not you were able to recall a problem experience clearly and write it out at the end of chapter 2, please make your best effort to provide brief, written answers to the following questions. The same advice still applies. Write quickly, without stopping to correct, by talking aloud and then writing down what you've just said.

1. *Distaste for writing:* describe your dislikes of writing. Do you find it typically difficult? Tiring?

_____

_____

_____

2. *Lack of time for writing:* talk about time as something that hampers your writing. Do you have too much, too little? Or is it just badly managed?

_____

_____

_____

3. *Lack of confidence:* do you feel good about yourself as a writer or are there doubts and fears that get in the way? Are you afraid of being uncovered as a "fraud" or of not being able to make real contributions?

_____

_____

_____

_____

4. ***Writing anxiety:*** write about the nervousness you've experienced while writing. How did it feel (e.g., queasy stomach, sweaty forehead)? Where were you when it happened? Is it likely to recur?

_____

_____

_____

_____

_____

5. ***Inability to start writing:*** recall times, particularly recent ones, when you had trouble starting. How did it feel? What did you do to help?

_____

_____

_____

_____

_____

6. ***Inability to finish writing:*** have there been times when you obsessed too long over a paper or some part of it? Or did you tend to ' the opposite extremes by attempting to finish with a single draft, or by not looking at what you'd written (and then having to face problems of submitting manuscripts with unnecessary errors)?

_____

_____

_____

_____

7. ***Other psychological disruptions:*** describe your experiences related to the following:

a. ***depression:*** do you tend to give up too easily, to be too sad and negativistic? What do you do to cope or get out of the negative mood?

_____

_____

_____

_____

_____

b. *phobic avoidance:* does your avoidance of writing go beyond the realistic aversiveness of writing? Do you hurt your personal and professional development by reflexively avoiding writing if you can?

_____

_____

_____

c. *cramping:* when pressured, do you try to write too quickly, so that your hand/wrist/arm tires easily? How do you cope when you feel yourself cramping?

_____

_____

_____

_____

Finally, transcribe your comments into a preliminary diagnosis on this rating form:

Rate your perception of how serious each factor is as a disruptor of your writing. Circle the part of the scale that best describes you:

	No problem		Serious problem
	0	5	10
1. Distaste for writing	|﹍|﹍|﹍|﹍|﹍|﹍|﹍|﹍|﹍|﹍|
	0	5	10
2. Lack of time for writing	|﹍|﹍|﹍|﹍|﹍|﹍|﹍|﹍|﹍|﹍|
	0	5	10
3. Lack of confidence	|﹍|﹍|﹍|﹍|﹍|﹍|﹍|﹍|﹍|﹍|
	0	5	10
4. Writing anxiety	|﹍|﹍|﹍|﹍|﹍|﹍|﹍|﹍|﹍|﹍|
	0	5	10
5. Inability to start writing	|﹍|﹍|﹍|﹍|﹍|﹍|﹍|﹍|﹍|﹍|

6. Inability to finish writing

```
0            5           10
|__|__|__|__|__|__|__|__|__|__|
```

7. Other psychological disruptions

a depression.

```
0            5           10
|__|__|__|__|__|__|__|__|__|__|
```

b. phobic avoidance

```
0            5           10
|__|__| |__|__|__|__|__|__|__|
```

c. cramping

```
0            5           10
|__|__| |__|__|__|__|__|__|__|
```

With all that finished, it's time for one more reflection. However you're feeling about your own problem styles, you may benefit from a simple exercise. Once writers have disclosed their problems and have made a simple assessment of them, they often take the written accounts of other blocked writers with them. When I see them next, they usually say that it helped to revisit reminders of other people's blocking experiences.

Your copies of such phenomenological accounts can be found, as you doubtless know, by reviewing this chapter. (Notice how professors like me enjoy checking to see if you're napping.)

Other questionnaires that permit even more formal assessments appear in Part 1 of the Appendices. They don't take long to complete. In earlier versions of this manual, I included the formal questionnaires in this chapter. But I learned that some readers were put off by the prospect of such a quantitative analysis. Now these self-assessments appear out of context.

If you choose to fill them out, you'll develop a sense of the dimensions of writing problems and of your relative position in them. Two kinds of distinctions are made. One represents modalities of writing problems.

1. overt signs (e.g., putting off writing as long as possible)
2. cognitions and emotions (e.g., "I feel nervous about starting")
3. social skills (e.g., "my friends take an active interest in my writing")

The other distinction concerns components of writing problems:[1]
1. work apprehension (e.g., "I don't feel like doing this")
2. procrastination (e.g., "I work best when I wait until the last minute")
3. writing apprehension (e.g., "I just don't match up to what others can do")
4. dysphoria (e.g., "I'm too depressed to write")
5. impatience (e.g., "I'm not working fast enough")
6. perfectionism (e.g., "What if someone finds a mistake in my paper?")
7. rules (e.g., "I hate to outline")

Characterizing writing blocks as having 21 facets (three modalities times seven components) may seem complicated. Actually, this scheme helps simplify a difficult topic into a manageable scheme. In many of the chapters that follow, I offer specific advice for people with specific profiles on these questionnaires.

Notes

[1]Research establishing these components of blocking includes Boice, R. (1985), Cognitive components of blocking. *Written Communication, 2*, 91-104.

SECTION B:
Strategies for the Short Run

Introduction

IF YOU'RE already writing, why bother practicing techniques for establishing momentum?

Because, for one thing, these techniques entail more than merely getting started. The next two chapters focus on techniques that begin with unthinking, "automatic" ways of generating useful ideas, ways of raising one's daily consciousness about writing, and ways of building conceptual outlines into rough drafts. This step-wise system can produce better writing, more writing, and quicker completion of projects.

Another good reason reflects the reality of writing for most of us. There will be days when we just don't feel like writing, days when the law of delay ("that which can be delayed, will be") dominates, days when we will feel devoid of ideas and competence. At those times it will help to know techniques that make us begin and that foster motivation, creativity, and competence–regardless of mood.

Chapter Four

Spontaneous Writing

ONCE UNDER WAY, writing builds its own momentum. But, until writing is under way, the act can seem foreign. Dorothea Brande, in her 1934 classic *Becoming a Writer*, put it simply: "First, there's the difficulty of writing at all."[1]

What makes beginning more difficult for some people than others? Answer: The same things that cause writing problems more generally, like perfectionism, operate here. And self-consciousness joins in.

Writing, much like drawing and talking, is aided by consciousness only in limited ways. Consciousness, the rational self-talk we engage in at times,[2] helps with preplanning and with editing tasks, for example. But consciousness hinders writing when it produces the self-awareness, the readiness to judge and blame, and obsessiveness.

Yogi Berra, the former baseball player, is credited with the most famous analysis of the problem: "You can't think and hit at the same time."

Similarly, writing often proceeds most smoothly and fluently when writers work without conscious reflection of what they're writing. When they do so, writers master a most important skill. They learn to write without feeling "ready," without feeling fully in control, without awaiting inspiration. They learn to proceed quickly and without looking back, perhaps because, as Virginia Woolf believed, writing at a gallop leaves one's internal critics behind. And they learn to tolerate imperfect material.

If you haven't mastered the strategy, you might wonder about the advantages of writing unselfconsciously and unselfcritically. It gets you started writing, regardless of mood. And it produces useful material for rewriting, some of it surprising. Composition teachers have a favorite saying that explains the benefit of writing for surprise: "How do I know what I think until I see what I write?"

Spontaneous Writing

Dorothea Brande didn't invent the technique; she merely helped popularize it. Her version, called effortless writing, reflects the greater emphasis, a half-century ago, of accessing the unconscious by working when not fully awake:

> The best way to do this is to rise half an hour, or a full hour, earlier than you customarily rise. Just as soon as you can–and without talking, without reading the morning's paper . . . Write anything that comes into your head . . . Write any sort of reverie, rapidly and uncritically. The excellence or ultimate worth of what you write is of no importance yet. As a matter of fact, you will find more value in this material than you expect, but your primary purpose now is not to bring forth deathless words but to write any words at all.[2] (pp. 72-73)

Done as directed, Brande assured readers, her strategy produces two related advantages: Effortless writing should reflect the rich, smooth unconscious processes it taps. And writing should no longer seem arduous or dull.

My experiences with professors as writers indicate that Brande was right. But many of my clients objected to one aspect of her prescription for establishing momentum. They were unwilling to get up even earlier in already long and demanding days.

My own version of effortless writing, then, emphasizes the rapid and uncritical style, whenever writers want to begin. While the records of productivity and creativity favor writers who work at writing during mornings, most people do relatively well at other times, even in the interstices of hectic schedules.

The result of my evolutionary experiences with effortless writing resembles many contemporary approaches to unself-conscious writing, notably Peter Elbow's "free writing."[3] I prefer the label of *spontaneous writing* for its self-descriptiveness and its much older historical links to Romantic poets like Wilhelm Ritter who used spontaneous thinking to generate creative work.[4]

Experiencing Spontaneous Writing

Nothing short of trying it suffices. If we were meeting directly, we would be in our third or fourth session and I'd say: "We've talked enough, for the moment. It's time to try some spontaneous writing." [And you might ask, with mild alarm, "now?"] "Right! Now! Nothing to it but writing rapidly and uncritically, writing anything that comes to mind."

Next, I'd give you a pencil and a copy of the Spontaneous Writing Sheet (SWS) that appears below. (Because spontaneous writing requires repeated trials, I hope you'll write on photocopies of the SWS.)

Spontaneous Writing Sheet (SWS)

Date _____ _____

Peter Elbow's (1973) instructions are clearest: "The idea is simply to write for ten minutes (later on, perhaps fifteen or twenty). Don't stop for anything. Go quickly without rushing. Never stop to look back, to cross something out . . . to wonder what word or thought to use, or to think about what you are doing. If you can't think of a word or a spelling, just use a squiggle or else write, 'I can't think of it.' Just put down something." (p. 1)

Then, I'd place my watch on the table, remind you that it will last only 10 minutes, and say "Ready?" You'll need to take over my function and simply prod yourself to begin.

Most professors then proceed, almost furiously, for 10 minutes of nonstop writing. When they don't, the conversation usually takes one of these forms:

[you] "I can't think of anything to say."

[me] "Oh, come on now, you just said something; try beginning with that. Really. Begin with whatever you're thinking and you'll soon be writing other things."

[you] "I'll feel stupid."

[me] "Maybe. But you'll undoubtedly survive. I won't laugh or be critical. Besides, you won't know until you try. The point is to let the momentum get you beyond your self-consciousness, including feeling that you might sound stupid."

[you] "It'll just be nonsense, a waste of my time. I need to get on with real writing."

[me] "I know how you feel. But, I'll bet that you'll have a hard time making your SWS exercise as worthless as you suppose. Consider this: You speak clearly and with substance when you express what's on your mind to me. Why shouldn't effortless writing produce similarly good stuff, stuff that you can even use in real writing?"

What if you still can't start? Then cheat.

Begin by copying a passage from a book, word for word. Or if you're cramped, have a friend transcribe what you say as you free-associate (while pausing and repeating if your friend is not a stenographer). Or use spontaneity to take notes on the literature relevant to your planned manuscript. Keep this up until you can make the transition—from copying, from rewording your friend's copy, from writing aloud or on paper, or from note taking—to your own spontaneous writing. Sooner or later, especially with help from a friend, you'll get it going.

Sharing Spontaneous Writing

This step is optional. But you'll probably be glad you did it. Practice spontaneous writing with a friend, colleague, someone. Then, without apologies or provisos, take turns reading your own SWSs aloud.

You'll be pleased, in my experience, with the sheer bulk of what you've written. You'll be surprised, if you reflect on it, how easy it was once you jumped into it. And, you'll be pleased at how well written much of it is. Unself-conscious writing tends to be simple and direct.

Most important, your listeners will probably like what they hear. Many of us, especially professionals, have nearly forgotten how to begin our evaluations of writing with compliments, but they'll come—and they can be genuine.

Being able to share imperfect writing with others is a critical step in making the writing truly effortless. Sharing imperfect copy helps demonstrate that writing need not be perfect to communicate well. Sharing imperfect copy helps build confidence, especially with compliments and encouragement from others. And sharing imperfect copy encourages effortless improvement, via rewriting and via sharing. When, in contrast, we share only finished writing with others, we really discourage their effective or enthusiastic inputs. I suspect that, despite claims to the contrary, authors of finished drafts do not welcome major revisions.

If you don't have someone with whom to share at this stage, use this typical first attempt at spontaneous writing by one of my clients for comparison:

> *I don't really know where to start. This writing does not come easily. My mind is blank. What should I write about? I really want to be a better writer. I guess that's why I'm doing this. Wouldn't it be nice if writing could be easy—if the words would just flow and I could feel good about my writing. Writing is very important to me yet it seems so difficult. When I came here today I really didn't expect to be writing like this. My mind is still blank this isn't going to be easy. I guess that is the way I usually start—feeling as though I have little to say and not knowing where to start. It really isn't a comfortable feeling. The harder I try the more difficult writing becomes. I want to relax while I'm writing. Next week I'm going to Switzerland for a vacation. I've never been there before. I'm going to visit some relatives. Perhaps while there I will feel more like writing.*

When you've read this example of spontaneous writing, ask yourself the following questions: What compliment would you address to this author knowing that, before starting, she expressed grave fears of writing stupid, nonsensical material? Are any of her ideas salvageable? Does it really matter in this first attempt? Then, comment on your own SWS in similar fashion.

Practicing Spontaneous Writing

Whether or not you're able to do "real" writing, continue to practice spontaneous writing in brief daily sessions of 10-15 minutes. You might enjoy this momentum-inducing strategy in the form of journal or diary writing.[5] You might find it easier to retell something you've just read or to write while speaking aloud to someone, real or imaginary. You might like rewriting your previous SWS.

Experiment. Find what works best for you to make getting started effortless.

Later, when you've moved on to more formal writing, the spontaneous technique can still play a vital role. I recommend that all writers practice beginning *each* daily session with five minutes of spontaneous, mindless writing. Doing so generates momentum and ideas. And having practiced it provides insurance against those days when getting started is difficult.

For the time being, plan to practice a maximum of 10-15 minutes a day of spontaneous writing, especially if you have problems with perfectionism and low self-confidence that make getting started difficult. Keep your productivity chart going; spontaneous writing at this stage should count as the kind of productivity that you display on your graph.

But, don't stay with spontaneous writing too long. After a week (two weeks at most) of no more than 10-15 minute sessions of spontaneous writing, move to the next chapter.[6]

Notes

[1]Brande, D. (1981). *Becoming a writer*. Los Angeles: J. P. Tarcher (reprint of the 1934 edition published by Harcourt, Brace).

[2]The popular, speculative, notion of consciousness and related, rational activities as reflections of left-brain hemisphere functioning is explained most provocatively in Jaynes, J. (1977), *The origin of consciousness in the breakdown of the bicameral mind*. Boston: Houghton Mifflin. An approach to unblocking that focuses on right-brain techniques is Rico, G. L. (1983), *Writing the natural way*. Los Angeles: J. P.

Tarcher. Some people prefer accounts of left-handed approaches to living and working, written before psychologists incorporated all the physiologizing about brain mechanisms. A favorite of mine: Bruner, J. (1962), *On knowing: Essays for the left hand.* Cambridge, MA: Harvard University Press. Another more recent view of the left-right brain metaphor is less sanguine. Promoters of hemisphericity tend to oversimplify and misrepresent the brain's actual functioning; in fact, for example, most people tend to use both hemispheres all the time. See Levy, J., (1985), Right brain, left brain: Fact and fiction. *Psychology Today, 19* (#5), 38-42.

[3]Elbow, P. (1973). *Writing without teachers.* New York: Oxford University Press.

Elbow, P. (1981). *Writing with power.* New York: Oxford University Press.

[4]See Haym, R. (1870). *Die romantische Schule.* Berlin: R. Gaertner.

[5]See Rainer, T. (1978), *The new diary: How to use a journal for self-guidance and expanded creativity.* Los Angeles: J. P. Tarcher.

[6]See Boice, R., & Myers, P. (1986), Two parallel traditions: Automatic writing and free writing, *Written Communication, 3,* 471-490, for warnings about practicing spontaneous writing for longer than 15 minutes.

Chapter Five

Generative Writing

> The results-first approach changes the whole psychology of performance improvement. . . . People must ask different kinds of questions. . . . not, "what is standing in the way?" but rather, "what are some things we can accomplish in the next little while?". . . . Instead of trying to overcome resistance to what people are *not* ready to do, find out what they are ready to do.[1]

THE QUOTE ABOVE comes from the best-selling book for executives, *In Search of Excellence*. When Thomas Peters and Robert Waterman wrote it, they could just as well have been talking about spontaneous writing. Their "Don't just stand there, do something!" approach describes what we've been doing; the point, after all, is to stop talking about resistance to writing and to discover what you *are* ready to do.[2]

If you're already practicing spontaneous writing (or spontaneous note taking), you're probably benefiting from the results-first approach. Your momentum should be growing. Your resistance should be diminishing. And, following the dictates of the results-first approach, you should be ready to consider why spontaneous writing works.

But, you might ask, if spontaneous writing already works, why bother to understand its mechanisms? Because, first of all, insights about spontaneous writing can perpetuate its effectiveness, especially if you relapse into blocking. And, second, spontaneous writing has limitations, even potential drawbacks. Learning more about spontaneous writing helps set the stage for moving on to its safer and more product-oriented relative, generative writing.

Historical Development of Spontaneous Writing

Heaven knows who invented spontaneous writing; it must be almost as old as rough, rough drafts. But information is available about some of the people who first popularized similar techniques. My favorite is Ludwig Borne's (1858) *Art of Becoming an Original Writer in Three Days*.[3] His prescription was simple (notice, he promised originality, not success): seclusion (three days' worth), plus doing little else but writing whatever came to mind. Borne's methods, especially his claims for releasing dangerously repressed words, influenced many writers, including Freud.[4] (However, I strongly advise you not to follow Borne's prescription, for reasons I'll discuss later.)

At about the same time, Mesmerists came to a conclusion that paralleled Borne's: People in trance-like states, who had blocked out most self-conscious awareness, could produce remarkably original writing and drawing. That is, they evidenced what was once known as "psychic automatism."[4] Eventually, as Mesmerism evolved into spiritualism (or spiritism), similar strategies were used to produce "automatic writers" whose novel outpourings were considered messages from the spirit world.

These parallel traditions, what Borne called original writing and what the spiritists called automatic writing, are progenitors of the spontaneous writing we have been practicing.

Automatic Writing: Popularization. Its greatest popularity came in an era when Americans were eager to read the prolific outpourings of automatic writers. Messages from the other side seemed to be transmitted by deceased poets and philosophers, even by inhabitants of Jupiter.[5]

Whether or not their accounts were valid, spiritists showed the potential of automatic writing as an unblocking technique. According to one report, an automatic writer produced 7 to 14 poems an hour, "rarely trivial in subject and without erasures."[6]

Early psychotherapists, at the turn of our century, recognized the value of automatic writing beyond spiritism, for revealing unconscious ideas. Pierre Janet, another important influence on Freud, used automatic writing as the first systematic projective technique. Morton Prince, a pioneer of abnormal psychology in America, promoted automatic writing for its spontaneity of expression and its freedom from self-conscious artifacts. And by mid-century, automatic writing had attracted other prominent supporters, Milton Erickson and Anita Muhl among them.[7]

Like other psychotherapeutic procedures associated with hypnosis, however, automatic writing sank into obscurity. Hypnosis in general acquired a reputation as a mysterious, potentially dangerous set of procedures that too often attracted charlatans as practitioners. Automatic writing gained specific ill repute as possibly addictive and as potentially destabilizing.

Automatic Writing: Methodology. It begins (in the format I typically use), as do most hypnotic procedures, by educating writers as to what should happen (e.g., novel, effortless writing) and by inducing a high level of suggestibility. Next, it narrows conscious attention so that the suggestion (of writing) can be effected. The writer sits at a table with pencil in hand, ready to write upon a piece of paper positioned off to the side—while resting his or her head/eyes in the crook of the non-writing arm. Then, the writing facilitator suggests that writing will begin.

To help ensure the writer's unawareness of what is being written, the writing facilitator (in early sessions, at least) reads aloud from something interesting like a novel.

Usually, writers begin writing on cue. Initial efforts may be indecipherable; some efforts resemble doodling. But with practice (and with the optional aid of a third person who coaches the writer's writing hand to write more legibly, within the page margins), readable copy appears. The results are typically dramatic. In my experience, all of the automatic writers wrote almost immediately and produced impressively good writing. Most achieved the unthinkable—good clear prose (or, in a few cases, good poetry), with no conscious effort.

All those writers agreed that they evidenced more skill in writing than they had supposed. All expressed a sense of having accessed their deep sources of creativity.

Automatic Writing: Pitfalls. So why, then, isn't automatic writing promoted more widely? In part, the experience doesn't always generalize readily to other, more normal writing experiences. Some of the people who got started writing in the trance state were disinclined to try it any other way.

The other part of the problem, though, is much more serious. A few people, despite warnings, began practicing it alone, without clinical supervision. One of them produced recollections of traumatic early experiences, long forgotten, that helped produce a temporary, but frightening depression. The same experience in a less emotionally stable person might have been even more problematic.

The third reason why automatic writing remains unpopular may be the most convincing: non-hypnotic equivalents, like Borne's "original writing" or Elbow's free writing, work nearly as well.

Original Writing: More Beginnings. The evolution of "original" writing into free writing and spontaneous writing included roots in automatic writing. William James, whose interests spanned spiritualism and research on multiple personalities, provided one link. He inspired a student, Gertrude Stein, to experiment on automatic writing as a test of what causes the dissociation of ideas in states like multiple personalities.[7] While their conclusion (that distraction caused the dissociation) was of little consequence, the *experience* was. Stein elaborated it into a technique she called "experimental writing" and into the creative style of writing that helped make her famous and influential.[8]

Her influence in Paris spread to famous writers such as Hemingway and to the artists and writers known as Surrealists.[9] They, like her, often wrote in defiance of rules of logical meaning (even of grammar, capitalization, and punctuation). And they, like her, wrote whole novels in a style they called automatic but that was clearly related to free writing.

Andre Breton, a hero of surrealism, gave these instructions:

> Attain the most passive or receptive state of mind possible. Forget your genius, your talents, and those of everyone else. . . . Write quickly with no preconceived subject, so quickly that you retain nothing and are not tempted to reread. Continue as long as you like.

Breton supposed that this procedure brought writers into contact with their innermost selves, the point from which creativity seems to flow. What made the surrealistic technique dissimilar from traditional automatic writing was apparent freedom from a hypnotist or hypnogogic state.[4] Presumably, writers merely needed to learn to be good observers of their "inner discourse" (intermittent short sentences or disconnected groups of words, carrying a flow of images, vying for supremacy).

Surrealists simply took dictation, inner dictation, by listening carefully and recording faithfully.

Original Writing: More Pitfalls. But, practiced in so intense a form by Surrealists, this form of automatic writing did put people into trances.[4] A few Surrealists evidently experienced mental instability as a result. The part of Breton's direction about continuing as long as you like may have been bad advice for some people.

What emerges in this historical account is a two-sided picture of spontaneous writing. Practiced in moderation, it works nicely to establish momentum and novelty in writing. Practiced to excess, without some supervision or clear constraints, it can produce upsetting revelations.

Legitimization. So it is, perhaps, that free writing did not attain widespread popularity and legitimacy until Peter Elbow established it as something to be practiced in brief sessions. His instructions, as you may recall from the top of the Spontaneous Writing Sheet (Chapter 4), include a directive about beginning with 10 minutes and an indication that its length thereafter is a matter of adding one or two five-minute blocks, not hours or days.

That directive alone, however, is not sufficient to explain Elbow's success. He also writes with unusual clarity and conviction:[10]

> Free writing makes writing easier by helping you with the root psychological or existential difficulty in writing: finding words in your head and putting them on a blank piece of paper.

He demonstrates his familiarity with the obstacles to free writing by anticipating the uncomfortable loss of control felt by some writers:

> The reason it feels like chaos and disorientation to write freely is because you are giving up a good deal of control.

And, he gives a good reason why free writing works:

> Free writing is the best way to learn in practice, not just in theory to learn to separate the producing process from the revising process.

That is, free writing teaches writers to delay editing and other parts of the revising process until writing is well under way. Our internal editors tend to get in the way if we let them start work too early.

Other Reasons Why Spontaneous Writing Works

In addition to Peter Elbow's favorite reason why spontaneous writing works (i.e., the very spontaneity of spontaneous writing helps us work around our internal critics), two others may be recalled from the historical account just completed. One reason can be associated with Surrealists who thought that automaticity accesses creative processes. The other reason seems most clearly identified with automatic writing. It, like other variants on writing unselfconsciously, gives people license to write without feeling responsibility for the product. That same license, of writing without conscious awareness, brings related freedoms, including the right to be playful and imperfect.

In other words, spontaneous writing works because it puts off our internal editor, taps creative processes, and allows suspension of responsibility. But how, exactly, does spontaneous writing bring about that delaying, that creativity, and that suspension?

The best answer to that question, surprisingly, comes from a drawing teacher.[11] Betty Edwards' popular book, *Drawing on the Right Side of the Brain*, doesn't even discuss writing. Nonetheless, it works effectively to teach writers several important lessons: It demonstrates new ways of seeing and representing things, via direct experience and then rational understanding. It builds insights about how spontaneity, combined with relaxed attentiveness, produces painless and skillful products. And, it ties these experiential insights into contemporary notions about brain mechanisms.

Consistent with Edwards' results-first approach, you might try one of her exercises before considering her rationale. Try drawing a portrait, freehand, from a picture. You'll probably have a rough time and the result will be unartistic. Then, start afresh with a blank page and with the photo inverted. Do your drawing upside down, beginning with lines at the top of the page.

The second method works *much* better because it's more spontaneous; you proceed with less inclination to name the parts you're drawing but with more inclination to attend to configurations.

Once you've tried such techniques for spontaneity, you may be better able to appreciate her explanation of why naming things gets us in trouble:

> From childhood onward, we have learned to see things in terms of words: we name things, and we know facts about them. The dominant left verbal hemisphere [of the brain] doesn't want much information about things it perceives–just enough to recognize and categorize. The left brain, in this sense, learns to take a quick look and says "Right, that's a chair (or an umbrella, bird, tree, dog, etc.)." Because the brain is overloaded most of the time with incoming information, it seems that one of its functions is to screen out a large proportion of incoming perceptions. . . . The left brain has no patience with this detailed perception, and says, in effect, "It's a chair, I tell you. That's enough to know. In fact, don't bother to look at it, because I've got a ready-made symbol for you". . . . When confronted with a drawing task, the left hemisphere comes rushing in with all its verbally linked symbols; afterward, ironically, the left brain is all too ready to supply derogatory words of judgment if the drawing looks childlike or naive.

Consider how Betty Edwards' understanding of blocking translates to writing. Ordinarily we allow our consciousness (the repository of rational, self-conscious thought) too much control when starting with writing. That is, the self-conscious mode of working emphasizes shortcuts, time urgency, labeling, and perfectionism. Then, after it has helped prevent you from getting started, it tells you what a pathetic job you're doing.

This is how consciousness works when it dominates writing:[12]

1. It produces self-consciousness.
2. It narratizes. It carries on a narrative, or story an abstracted account of what is happening to you. Narratives often incorporate memories of the past and expectations of the future. Consciousness often brings worrying.
3. It assigns causes and effects in its stories. Consequently, it blames. It also obsesses and criticizes; given free rein, consciousness may tend to exaggerate, even to distort causes and effects.
4. It provides a sense of time, another essence of consciousness. It can also produce a sense of time urgency.

No wonder, then, that conscious mechanisms are implicated in writing problems. And, no wonder that unself-conscious mechanisms are so widely prescribed as means of getting writers started. Here are some characteristics of spontaneous styles of working:

1. You are more or less unconscious, much as you are for periods of time when you're driving on a freeway; you realize, upon regaining consciousness, that you were attending to driving but that nothing much was happening mentally. In this state, you're assured of not being self-conscious.

2. You don't narratize in the sense of carrying on an accounting of what is going on around you. You can attend, instead, with remarkable exclusivity to the task at hand (e.g., dancing, even writing).

3. You abandon blaming, worrying, and criticizing.

4. You essentially lose your awareness of time.

All these unself-conscious phenomena occur when spontaneous writing is done properly. They happen, evidently, because techniques like spontaneous writing demand a shift away from usual conscious dominance to the more easygoing, intuitive, emotional, configurational style of unself-conscious dominance. After you've mastered the art of shifting to spontaneous modes, you'll understand why some people call it the Zen of writing.

So, when you're getting started, at least, it may be best not to try to think and write at the same time.

Why Spontaneous Writing Fails

Spontaneous writing fails when we try to extend its simple functions (teaching ways to shift brain dominance, ways to get started writing, ways to produce novel material) too far.

Sometimes, the problem originates in the ease and enjoyment of spontaneous writing. The new experience of writing so painlessly, so copiously may be such an improvement that a return to other kinds of writing feels aversive. Spontaneous writing may, if carried too far, become compartmentalized–a kind of writing where one has fun but seemingly accomplishes nothing of relevance to real-life writing tasks. Carried even further, it can produce the emotional upheavals discussed earlier.

In my experience, writers in general (particularly non-starters and perfectionists) have trouble making the transition from spontaneous writing to writing that can be revised into useful copy.[13] Even some of the most patient people begin to worry about when and how they can move past the disarray of spontaneous writing to something more on target.

One solution involves bringing the conscious mind back into adaptive action. As is so often true, too much of a good thing (even the liberating influence of the spontaneity) can be bad. Consider, as a preliminary example, the case of classroom teaching. In my research on faculty development, I've observed many teachers and have confirmed something you may have suspected: most teachers are far too self-conscious; they bore and fatigue students with endless facts, lists, and explanations. The best teachers, as a rule, include occasional spontaneous strategies such as telling anecdotes.

Students like anecdotes. When listening to most anecdotes, they relax, rest their writing hands, and assume a far-off look. Moreover, they remember anecdotes and the factual material relating to anecdotes.

But students don't like (or benefit much from) lectures that consist almost entirely of anecdotes. They prefer a balance. Our minds seem to be engineered to work best at jobs like listening to lectures or writing when we're not locked too long in either side.

Still, you should be skeptical. The conscious mind can do horrible things, including making you apprehensive and self- critical. Fortunately for us, that popular characterization of the "left brain" represents only part of the picture–its functioning at the worst, most undisciplined level. In fact, consciousness has real advantages:

1. It permits reading. (Notice, when you're dreaming and therefore in a nearly complete state of right-brained dominance, how unlikely you are to read–*actually* read the words on the page you're dreaming of.) Without reading, writing would be as pointless as the prospect of learning better ways of writing.

2. The rational mind allows self-observation and evaluation of ongoing activities with an eye to improved action.

3. It encourages short-cutting, ways of solving problems, of making connections, of establishing plans.

4. It occasions a sense of self, of self-worth, and of special enjoyment in consciously planned achievements including writing. It also al-

lows, via a sense of self, a sense of audience, of how others will probably respond to what we say or write.

So, when it isn't allowed to run amuck, the conscious mind can provide many valuable services. Its particular strength in related areas of planning, of problem solving, and of developing a sense of audience indicates why, once spontaneous writing is under way, it should be brought back into play for a consultation.

I call this second step, of adding planning and direction to already established spontaneity, *generative writing*. I mean generative in the sense of working toward useful copy, with some loosely defined goals in mind–but still writing with little concern for perfection.

Generative writing works in alternating fashion, relying on both sides of the mind, until the copy approaches a complete first draft. Practiced properly, generative writing helps make the transition from pure spontaneity to producing useful copy almost painless. At first, of course, generative writing can hurt. The spontaneous mind, neglected as it typically is, hates to give up the floor.

Generative Writing

Perhaps you sense what I'll say next. With my fondness for the results-first approach, I'd prefer to have you try generative writing before you think much more about it. First, the unself-conscious mind, then the conscious mind.

First Approximation: GWS-I

Initially, generative writing closely resembles spontaneous writing. It begins with an almost identical format. The Generative Writing Sheet (GWS-I) on the following page is used much as was the SWS of Chapter 4 (including the recommendation that you work on photocopied sheets). The instructions, though, are different in one striking way. Now, although you're asked to write without stopping or editing, etc., you're asked to write with a specific topic in mind. You'll write about some critical or memorable point in your education where you were encouraged or discouraged, helped or hindered, in your writing.

You may be surprised. It still goes quickly; most people can easily recall such an experience and they simply start writing the story as it comes to mind. It's much the same as the spontaneous writing you've already practiced; you'll be able to write surprising amounts, but you'll stay on topic and the story will have an ending (even if you don't reach it in 10 minutes).

Date _____

Generative Writing Sheet I (GWS-I)

Pause just long enough to recall an experience from your school years that helped or hindered your writing. Then, before you've had a chance to think it all out, begin writing it spontaneously. Stick to the story, but don't stop for anything. Go quickly without rushing. Don't struggle over form or correctness. Just get something down. Keep it up for 10 minutes.

_____

_____

_____

_____

_____

_____

_____

_____

_____

The Experience of Generative Writing in First Approximation

Just as with old-fashioned spontaneous writing, nothing short of trying it suffices. And, as before, some people still need to clear up hesitancies:

[you] "I can't think of a story."

[me] "Really? You can't recall a single time when you worked on a writing project in school?"

[you] "Well, I think I can, but I'm not sure how well I can remember it."

[me] "That's good enough. Just get started and you may find that it'll come to you as you proceed. If not, you can write about how odd it is that you have no ready memories of this sort and what that might mean. The main thing is to make a beginning, to take the risk of beginning before you feel you're ready. Let the writing process do some of the work for you."

[you] "I can think of a story but it's not a very good one."

[me] "What's wrong with it?"

[you] "It really isn't very significant or original."

[me] "That's all right. You're not obliged, particularly at this point, to be clever or original. Just share an experience. You might want to include commentary about how commonplace or uneventful it seems. You could even consider what difference more interesting experiences would have made for you as a writer. But for heaven's sake, don't pressure yourself by supposing that you can't begin unless you already have something impressive to say. Let that take care of itself, as you generate and revise material. The point now is to make a beginning. You may profit even more by insisting, for now, on an imperfect beginning."

[you] "I'd rather take more time to think about it, to plan it out. Then I could begin writing it as a real manuscript. This generative writing is fine for someone who has time to waste, but I like to get right down to work."

[me] "I think I know how you feel. At least try it. You may find that it provides a useful way of generating ideas, ideas that might not emerge via typical planning. You'll probably find, when you apply generative writing to your own writing ideas, that this method can help speed the completion of manuscripts. One advantage here is that you can begin before you feel ready. Once you begin, you'll be much more likely to carry out related tasks like literature searches, data analyses, discussions with prospective publishers, than you would have been if you hadn't already begun. In my experience, generative writing saves time."

[you] "It still seems like I'll feel silly."

[me] "Perhaps. But it probably won't hurt you. Instead, you may benefit by learning to tolerate a little more chaos and surprise in the writing process. Sometimes it's necessary to give up some control to acquire even more important kinds of control."

If you still can't get started, begin by reverting to something you know you can do, spontaneous writing. If nothing else, begin by writing about how blocked you feel. Then, once in motion, write about how little you have to say about the topic of schoolroom writing. If that proves too uncomfortable, revert to fully spontaneous writing. But continue to write for 10 minutes. Continue to come back to confrontations with the more structured topic. Sooner or later, even if you have to work while talking your story aloud to a friend, you'll be able to master generative writing.

Sharing Generative Writing. Here, as with spontaneous writing, you'll benefit more by working in a small group of supportive, uncritical people. You'll be more likely to begin because they're beginning. You'll be more likely to feel good about your writing when you've read it aloud in a context where others have read theirs and where everyone shares a sense of relief and tolerance.

This sample of generative writing from a professor in one of my workshops on writing may serve a similar purpose for writers working alone:

My inability to feel comfortable with writing seems to begin with undergraduate school. There I wrote only 3 papers, none of which where all that academic. Further, I never expected to be a graduate student and therefore never really worked at the development of the writing skills necessary. After entering graduate school I felt so far behind other students that again I did as little writing as possible. It seems to me that this further enforced the feelings of lack of writing skill to the point that I for the most part turned down opportunities to work of scholarly publications with people. I leaned instead to the development of computer skills that didn't require me to write. When people ask me to write & encourage me to write, I have been able to avoid it. My real problem may be a lack of self-confidence. This is perpetuated by lack of experience. Further complications have arise by a finely tuned system of avoidance behaviors that to most people make my lack of writing seem reasonable and therefore let up on pressure & stop pushing me in that direction. Overall, I tend to be very organized yet not in writing. Perhaps the creative nature of writing has scared me away. I feel so.

Having read this excerpt, think of how you might compliment the author. Did she, despite her initial doubts, generate an interesting story and even some useful copy for subsequent revisions? Then, comment on your own GWS-I in similar fashion.

Second Step: GWS-II

Most writers, in my experience, do better with generative writing when they change its topical heading to assignments of their own. Even so, the writers with whom I work often struggle at this point.

If, as is often the case, they're already bogged down in a writing project that seems well past the generative stage, how, they ask, can this be of any use? My answer typically goes like this:

• "For the moment, I'd like you to try it on faith. That's what the results-first approach requires. Later, you'll probably see that generative writing is valuable in reworking nearly finished papers, especially those needing revision. But for now, I'd like you to try generative writing to begin generating a *new* writing project."

The word "new" seems to generate the most resistance. Perhaps we might then interact as follows:

[you] "I don't have a new project I want to start right now. I want to finish the one that has gone unfinished for so long."

[me] "You probably will finish it, but with a bit of patience you can learn ways to make its completion easier. And you can learn to work on two, preferably three, projects simultaneously, in various stages of completion. Sometimes it's nice to add brief projects so that you have more frequent experiences in completing writing. Sometimes, working on just one writing project produces burnout. Being able to alternate between tasks helps keep writing fresher."

[you] "That's fine for you to say, but I just don't have anything else ready yet. I'd have to do a lot of literature searching, go back and read my notes, think about it before I could start. And, I'd rather put that off until I've finished what I'm working on now."

[me] "I understand. Just to humor me, though, give me an idea of what you will write about when you're ready to begin that project. Then, in my experience, you'll produce a fairly cogent description of what it will be about. Try it."

[me] "You see, you do have a sense of how you could begin to develop that project. Even though you don't feel ready. I think you might be pleasantly surprised if you began doing some generative writing on the new topic. You could devote part of each writing session to generating this project. And then you'd be much more likely to begin attendant tasks like checking out literature sources. Wouldn't it be neat to use generative writing to build momentum each writing day—momentum that would spill over into the writing project you've been working on, momentum that would also generate the new project long before you would otherwise have begun it?"

Perhaps, then, either worn out by my talkativeness or inspired about possible benefits, you'd be ready for GWS-II (page 62). The only real differences from GWS-I are these: the topical assignment is yours, and the story may not present itself in such completed form. Moreover, this may be a slower, reflective process than the spontaneous writing with which you began.

Then, when you've given GWS-II a try, do things you've already
done with the SWS and GWS-I exercises. Practice it. Share it. And
give yourself as much credit as a sympathetic listener would. Then,
practice it some more, using topics akin to your own writing projects.

You'll probably notice that generative writing produces experiences consistent with what we've already seen about inserting a bit of
consciousness into writing. The result is writing that proceeds somewhat more slowly and deliberately.

Date_____

Generative Writing Sheet II (GWS-II)

Reflect briefly on a new writing project you'd like to develop. But
don't reflect for long; you can always try another possibility in your
next trial. Then begin writing. Go quickly if you have ideas readily
available. Go slowly when you're thinking about directions, goals, audience, etc. But keep going. Don't struggle over form or correctness.
Just make a beginning. Keep it up for at least 10 minutes, for up to an
hour if you're generating good, on-topic material.

_____

_____

_____

_____

_____

_____

_____

_____

Third Step: GWS-III

Generative writing may seem less chaotic, less pointless than spontaneous writing, but it still feels separated from ordinary manuscript writing experiences. What comes next, then, helps facilitate the transition; it involves learning ways to transform generative writing into closer and closer approximations of a rough draft.

In GWS-III, I ask you to reread GWS-II and use it to generate a conceptual outline from what you've written. That is, sketch an informal diagram of the three or four main points that emerged (or would if you had written longer). Try doing it on the GWS-III format that appears on the next page.

The GWS-III format is intended *only* for a first approximation. You'll probably be more comfortable with your own, roomier work sheets. The important thing is to try it before you pause to recall how much you've always disliked outlining.

Generative Writing Sheet III (GWS-III)

This step of generative writing begins with *clustering*, a relatively unself-conscious way of developing a sense of organization in what you wrote in GWS-II. It is a nonlinear way of arranging the ideas in what you've written around one to four nuclear words.[14] One good way to work is by encircling the words, putting them in "balloons" and drawing arrows between the balloons. If you work quickly, without stopping to criticize or correct, you can take advantage of the spontaneous mind's ability to perceive connections and designs. With practice, clustering even helps writers discover subtle things, including a "voice" for a manuscript.

Then, after you've made a cluster diagram, switch to a more conscious mode of rearranging the points into a linear, logical arrangement (i.e., *listing*). Next, add brief, written approximations of what the points mean. Stop to correct, to add and delete. Reflect on whether the organization has a clear flow, makes the point you want to make, and will meet your audience's needs/expectations.

This stage of generative writing may not seem much like writing, but it is clearly generative. And it quickly leads back to more familiar forms of writing. Combined, the two phases of conceptual outlining in GWS-III (clustering and logical ordering) help provide a greater sense of direction, and less concern about chaos in generative writing.

With practice, conceptual outlining becomes more obviously linked to the writing that precedes and follows it. That is, when generating actual sentences and paragraphs, you'll be more likely to think of how your writing will translate into clusters and linear arrangements of points. And, when clustering and listing, you'll be more likely to think of new ways to state your points and of new connections between them. Writing, even in generative stages, works in circular fashion; the more you practice it, the more its processes work in harmony.

Fourth Step: Alternating Between GWS-II & GWS-III

No more new sheets. Now it's a matter of reusing GWS-II and GWS- III (or your own versions) to build progressively more length and substance into your new writing project.

I generally advise writers working on what will be 20-40 page manuscripts to follow a schedule like this: they can do generative writing in sessions of 20-30 minutes, each work day for 2-3 weeks. (The rest of their daily writing times may be devoted to other writing projects; we'll get back to that in the next chapter.)

The plan begins with already familiar steps:

1. Warm up, if necessary, with 5 minutes of spontaneous writing.
2. Begin generative writing (use GWS-II) with a topic in mind. Notice the reversal of usual writing practices: write first, then outline.
3. Use a GWS-III format to discover the design or pattern in what you've written, a design that will help direct subsequent revisions of your writing in new trials with the GWS-II.
4. Look over both the GWS-II and GWS-III, put them beside a new copy of GWS-II for reference, and begin a revision of what you wrote before. Because you're rewriting to some extent, this trial may go more quickly. And, the writing may be more finished. Don't try for perfectionism, though; let it happen on its own.

Because you're reworking something you've already had time to consider and design, you may write much more material than in the first GWS-II. Again, don't push. You probably won't need to finish in one sitting. It's nice to have the luxury of working patiently, with room for unrushed revisions.

5. Each time that you've completed a generative draft of a substantial portion of your project, stop to complete another GWS-III. Conceptual outlining acts to check direction, voice, and audience. It can also help with something else: you may see that you're trying to do too much, working in too much detail, making your project impractically and unreadably long.

6. When you've completed a generative draft that represents the whole of your intended project (and it's O.K. to have a number of "gaps" still existing), then start the manuscript over from the beginning. Stay away from format sheets like GWS-II and GWS-III, but don't lose sight of their mechanisms. Work on ordinary writing sheets (or on a typewriter or word processor if you prefer–but I advise carrying out these early stages in longhand). Work on manageably short sections, one at a time, in order. Don't skip around–doing so can diminish an essential feeling of continuity in your writing.

Write the first section or subsection. Stop to conceptually outline it to see if you're on track. Extend the outline to include the next few sections. Then, write the next section. Stop to outline what you've written (including the preceding section or sections) and extend the outline again to coming sections. Don't be tempted to reuse the extended outlines you've already constructed. Don't fall prey to the false belief that once in motion you no longer need to stop and incorporate conceptual outlining. You may be right if you're already an experienced, talented writer; even then you might need to revert to this step-wise approach at some troublesome point in your writing. Do, however, indulge the temptation to rewrite some sections (within limits). Some of the writers with whom I work like to rewrite the first, opening section each time they begin the next two or three sections as a means of clarifying their "voice" in a paper.

7. Finally, transform the combined generative drafts into one, continuously (and consciously) written manuscript. This may be a good time to violate the time-management principles I discuss later, especially my advice about writing in regular but moderate amounts. Stay at it. But don't let writing become so fatiguing that you won't feel like returning soon.

Remember that this is still an approximation to what we ordinarily call a first draft. Don't worry about perfection in writing style or about the gaps in scholarship or analyses that still exist. They'll get taken care of during the final revisions (even earlier, probably, because you may be too compulsive to let them stand for long). Don't worry, finally, if closure or a good ending hasn't appeared yet; they, too, tend to take care of themselves with time and patience.

Not all of this, of course, may be manageable in the two or three weeks in which I usually emphasize generative writing. The point is to get started. We'll continue to use generative writing as we add other structures and techniques to help ensure progress and success.

For the moment, while you're still practicing generative writing, pause to reconsider things in terms of the self-diagnosis you made earlier.

Individualized Problems and Generative Writing

Overall Blocking

Generative writing works to teach ways of coping with several aspects of writing problems: It helps you get unstuck by teaching ways of beginning before you're ready, of beginning before internal critics can set in, of generating ideas relevant to your topic, and of generating confidence.

This technique, along with the technique of contingency management (Chapter 6), is one of the two most critical agents in overcoming writing problems.

Perfectionism

Generative writing helps establish tolerance for imperfection. By definition, writing before you're ready means that you'll be writing imperfect sentences, leaving gaps in information/analysis, and taking pressure off yourself.

If you can share your generative writing with others, you'll help deal with another problem in perfectionism: you'll be forced to abandon some of your potential for elitism by allowing others to see your work in casual form.

Yet another benefit derives from sharing: you'll learn that others are rarely so demanding and critical as you might have expected that they can appreciate you for an idea, or even for the social act of communicating.

Writing Apprehension

Anxieties about writing resemble social anxieties in two critical ways: both require exposure plus knowledge about appropriate skills. Anxious writers need to begin by building some confidence about abilities to behave appropriately (i.e., generate some useful writing) and then they need to plunge into real-life tasks (i.e., writing assignments). Generative writing helps with both aspects. Experience in writing painlessly and competently builds confidence. Exposure to increasingly demanding writing tasks makes anxiety less likely, particularly as writers experience control over the moderate anxieties that may arise.

Writing Impatience

Nothing works better, in my experience, than generative writing for teaching the benefits and discipline of slowing down to do better work. By proceeding in step-wise fashion, without the prospect of finishing immediately, you short-circuit temptations to rush for completion in one or a few sessions.

Sharing generative writing is especially valuable for impatient writers. It helps build tolerance of criticism because sharing necessitates listening and responding. It helps ensure (if a supportive, constructive format is used) learning ways to give criticisms to other writers in a style that won't seem abrasive. And, slowing down to give and receive criticisms helps with another problem of many impatient writers: a deficient sense of audience.

Practicing generative writing establishes a most valuable experience/insight for impatient writers. It shows that a regimen of regular writing, in easy and sequential steps, produces more and better writing than working in frenzied binges.

Writing Dysphoria

Whatever else it does, generative writing provides a safe format in which to deal with the overwhelming aspects of writing. Because it demands staying on topic, generative writing discourages the surprising self-disclosures that can occur with extended spontaneous writing. Because it begins with small, manageable units of work, generative writing does not present overly demanding assignments. And because it encourages imperfect writing, generative writing reduces pressures to seem clever, original, and perfect.

Finally, generative writing can, especially in its earliest stages, be kept as private as you like; you may wish to delay the sharing exercises mentioned earlier until you've become comfortable with your writing. But don't wait too long (delaying unreasonably is, after all, a kind of writing problem).

Writing Rules

Generative writing, because it encourages new strategies (e.g., writing first, then outlining) and builds new perspectives, helps develop more flexibility in writing. Writers with rigid rules are, in my experience, most likely to reject the notion of generative writing. Curiously, they may benefit more from this procedure than most other problem writers.

Work Apprehension Score

The reason that I recommend generative writing to all writers is simple: it helps make writing painless. As you practice generative writing techniques, production of manuscripts becomes more automatic, less demanding. It's nice to have begun a writing project before you were ready, to have shaped it along (perhaps as an aside to some advanced project), and to find that you have a rough draft in hand–all without having felt much fatigue or apprehension.

Notes

[1]Peters, T. J., & Waterman, R. H. (1984). *In search of excellence: Lessons from America's best-run companies.* New York: Warner.

[2]Peters and Waterman review the classic debate between psychologists who believe that attitudes (beliefs, policies, proclamations) properly precede actions and those who believe that you are more likely to act yourself into feeling.

[3]Borne, L. (1858). *Gesammelte Schriften*. Milwaukee: Bickler.

[4]Ellenberger, H. (1970). *Discovery of the unconscious*. New York: Basic Books.

[5]Bois, J. (1907). *Le miracle modern*. Paris: Ollendorf.

[6]Gardiner, N. H. (1908). The automatic writing of Mrs. Holland. *Journal of the American Society for Psychical Research, 2*, 595- 626.

[7]See, for more details of methodologies and references concerning automatic writing, Boice, R., & Myers, P. (1986), Two parallel traditions, automatic writing and free writing. *Written Communication, 3*, 471-490.

[8]For an interesting criticism of Gertrude Stein's style and claims for originality, see Skinner, B. F. (1934), Has Gertrude Stein a secret? *Atlantic Monthly*, January, 359-369.

[9]Rainer, T. (1978). *The new diary*. Los Angeles: J. P. Tarcher.

[10]Elbow, P. (1973). *Writing without teachers*. New York: Oxford University Press.

[11]Edwards, B. (1979). *Drawing on the right side of the brain*. Los Angeles: J.P. Tarcher.

[12]Jaynes, J. (1978). *The origin of consciousness in the breakdown of the bicameral mind*. Boston: Houghton Mifflin.

[13]Both Brande and Elbow do discuss ways to move beyond the first stage. Brande lists techniques such as the "story in embryo" and "five-finger exercises." Elbow talks enthusiastically but vaguely about strategies such as "an emerging center of gravity" and "cooking as interaction between ideas." Having worked with hundreds of individuals and workshops who had tried free writing before I saw them, I conclude that few had moved beyond the kind of quick and painless writing that had no obvious transfer to scholarly or other formal writing projects.

[14]Rico, G. L. (1983). *Writing the natural way*. Los Angeles: J. P. Tarcher.

SECTION C:
A Regimen for Productive and Painless Writing: Strategies for the Long Run

Introduction

W E HAVE CONTINUED to follow the same plan I use with writers I see directly for writing blocks: We began with diagnoses of writing problems, with a preliminary sense of how those assessments relate to individualized programs. We moved next to strategies for establishing momentum in the short run; i.e., spontaneous writing and generative writing. The former, to echo Dorothea Brande, helps with the difficulty of writing at all. The latter helps direct the writing process beyond spontaneity, to the generation of more useful, disciplined material.

This section of our step-wise program completes the mechanics, or techniques, essential to a lasting, satisfying style of writing. Chapter 6 outlines ways to make writing a regular and productive habit via techniques based in established research; i.e., ways of arranging writing environments and writing habits to ensure writing as a high priority activity. Chapter 7 represents much newer developments in my research on helping problem writers. It extends to two older techniques, of making writing automatic and habitual, to techniques more concerned with the cognitive and social aspects of writing. These last two stages are deemed necessary to help move many writers beyond a grudging output of useful writing to writing that is also self-controlled and enjoyable.

Chapter Six

Ensuring Regular Productivity

GENERATIVE WRITING, despite its clear advantages, has a limitation: It doesn't *ensure* regular writing. Once the novelty of generative writing wears off, once disruptions such as personal traumas or busy work schedules occur, writing often gets put aside.

When I first point out this limitation to writers, many respond as follows:

- "Well, that's all right. I'd rather write when I'm in the mood."

I usually agree, to an extent; it might be nice if writing always came easily, spontaneously. But, then, I add a caution:

- "In reality, even the most experienced, productive writers often need to force themselves to write, regardless of mood.[1] Once under way, then *build* a positive mood, even an inspiration, for writing.[2] Try looking at it in another way: Sometimes I have to force myself to teach a lecture class; I'm not always in the mood. But once I'm teaching, I invariably discover that I'm enjoying it and doing it well. Teachers or writers who await mood and inspiration before beginning court trouble. Conversely, writers and teachers who create mood and inspiration by performing on demand tend to prosper."

Next, when we've shared experiences that corroborate this version of the results-first approach, I add another caution about putting off writing:

- "Waiting to write until there is enough 'free time' usually means that writing gets put off. In other words, it gets procrastinated. Except, perhaps, when deadlines loom directly ahead, writing is an activity that can always be put off. In my experience, the longer writing is put off, the more difficult it is to restart and the more likely that writing problems will recur."

Writing regardless of mood, in contrast, keeps momentum going. Writing regularly, even in moderate amounts, minimizes warm-up effects. Writing in a regimen produces both ease of writing and surprising output of writing.

When I've said all that, even if I'm communicating at my best, most of the writers with whom I work answer with a moment of silence. Then, they respond like this:

- "You may be right. But it feels like I would be giving up control of my writing. I don't want to be a writing machine. I would like to have my writing flow naturally."

What usually happens next fascinates me. When I've recounted case histories of writers who inevitably learned to enjoy writing on a regular schedule–even after I've reviewed my research showing that regular writing usually makes writers more spontaneous and creative[2] – a deeper skepticism emerges. Many writers then suppose that writing regularly means unreasonable sacrifices in life-style and in other work patterns.

One writer experiencing that skepticism brought a newspaper clipping[3] that confirmed her worst suspicions about productive writers. Its author had interviewed people who manage both successful careers and writing and found that they do have a secret: They sit down and write. "Of course they do," scoffed the writer. "That doesn't help." And then, with an indignant flourish she pointed out a photograph in the article. A successful "dual careerist" was pictured writing on a lap desk during a New York City cab ride. "If that's what it takes," she exclaimed, "forget it!"

Fortunately, that isn't what it takes for me or for any of the writers with whom I've worked. All of us have managed to be productive by devoting brief daily periods, sometimes no more than 30 minutes a day, to writing. Moreover, in my experience, this regimen requires giving up neither essential nor enjoyable activities. It never requires having to write during cab rides.

What learning to write regularly, painlessly, and productively does requires is the usual sacrifices of the results-first approach: a) suspension of skepticism, and b) willingness to plunge in and try it.

This time, though, the plunge needn't seem so drastic. We can put off the actual experience until we've paused to consider some rules and some evidence. Rules, incidentally, seemingly have some appeal to our spontaneous minds and, so, help make the transition to the results-first approach easier.

The Priority Principle

The most familiar rule about getting writing done is this one:

THE LAW OF DELAY: That which can be delayed, will be.

Generally, the law of delay is presented humorously. It sounds like a convenient and lovable excuse for a variety of misbehaviors.

But, as with most humor, a serious message lurks beneath. The law of delay not only says that things like writing, because they can be put off, will be put off. It also implies that you might as well accept the inevitability of delaying writing. It encourages passivity.

The trouble with finding a useful substitute for the law of delay is that the result is neither so humorous nor so memorable. However, the substitute does offer a solution to procrastinating:

THE PRIORITY PRINCIPLE: That which can be delayed, need not be. Decide which recurrent, daily activities you enjoy and make them contingent on doing a valued but delayable task first.

In other words, you can ensure the performance of highly valued tasks like writing by requiring their daily occurrence before more recurrent activities like a daily shower. No writing, no shower.

The priority principle simply says that if you're not writing as much as you would like, you're not making writing a realistic priority. If not writing means not being able to take a shower (or whatever daily activity you can give up without endangering yourself and others), then writing gains.

Some writers can ensure regular writing with a lower "priced" contingency such as letter writing or phone conversations. Other writers need to make the cost of not writing so high that they cannot afford to miss a writing session.[4] For example, some of the writers with whom I work request a contingency plan whereby a failure to write on any prescheduled writing day means that a prewritten check for $25.00 gets sent to a hated organization. Very few checks get mailed. These writers learn to write regularly regardless of initial mood.

Not surprisingly, many writers dislike the priority principle at first glance. It often seems too controlling and too superficial. And even where its practicality is admitted, it nonetheless promises to strain already overloaded schedules. That's why the priority principle works best with a results-first approach; only when you've gotten past the rational objections and into the experience can you see how well it works. Only then will you feel a sense of added control over writing, by virtue of working in disciplined fashion. Only then will you appreciate who the real agent of change is: you.

Stimulus Control Procedures

Although rearranging priorities may be the most essential step, related ways of rearranging your writing environment and habits also help ensure writing.

"Stimulus control" procedures, as behavioral psychologists call them, include anything that increases the probability of writing occurring regularly and successfully. (The priority principle qualifies as a stimulus control by definition.) My experience and research with writers suggest the following sets of guidelines:

Rearranging the Writing Environment

1. Establish one or a few *regular* places in which you will do all serious writing. If possible, make these locations (e.g., a desk in your study) places where you do nothing but serious writing; other writing (e.g., correspondence) would be carried out elsewhere.
2. Regular writing sites must also be sacred in the sense that no other temptations such as magazines, newspapers, novels can be on site. Thus, non-essential reading would be done elsewhere.
3. Similarly, the temptation of cleaning up one's writing site should not be allowed to distract. Instead, clean the writing area only at the completion of each session.
4. Arrange writing sites to minimize noisome distractions. Find a reasonably quiet place. Work with background music if it helps.
5. Limit social interruptions during writing times by: a) closing the door to your office, den, or whatever; b) posting a writing schedule on your closed door that requests visitors to limit interruptions to

brief (e.g., 10 seconds), essential messages;[5] c) unplugging the phone; and d) enlisting significant others and colleagues as enforcers by asking them to help head off potential disruptions (including, of course, themselves).

6. Enlist another writer to share part of your writing schedule by joining you for mutually quiet periods of work.

7. Make your writing site comfortable. I, for example, work best in a recliner chair because it reduces fatigue, especially neck and arm strain. Experiment to see what works best for you.

Rearranging Writing Habits

1. With the aid of the priority principle, make writing a daily activity, regardless of mood, regardless of readiness to write. Make a more regular, recurrent activity (e.g., phone calls to friends) contingent on writing for a minimum period of time first.

2. If you feel you have no time for regular writing, begin by charting your daily activities for a week or two in half-hour blocks. You may discover that you're "wasting" time on non-essential activities. For example, I've worked with teachers who, even with courses they had taught before, set aside an hour or two to reprepare each lecture. By limiting preparations to 30 minutes, they discovered that they went into class less over prepared, less rushed to cover the masses of material that would otherwise have been added, and more inclined to slow down and let students be more involved in the class. Results: higher student ratings and more time for writing.

3. Write while you're fresh. Schedule other, less mentally demanding tasks for times of the day when you're less alert and energetic. If evenings are a time when you're often tired, carry out other, less demanding tasks like correspondence and bill-keeping then.

4. Avoid writing in binges. Abandon the notion that writing is best done in large, undisrupted blocks of time. Waiting for such times does more than reinforce procrastination; it demands excessive warm-up times and it encourages you to write until you are fatigued.

5. Write in small, regular amounts. If you're writing regularly, 30-minute sessions may be adequately productive. Resist the tempta-

tion to extend normal sessions into binges that leave you feeling burned out on writing.

6. Schedule writing tasks so that you plan to work on specific, finishable units of writing in each session. For example, plan to complete a two-page conceptual outline or two pages of generative writing in a session. Some of the advantages of specifying writing tasks for each session are: a) you'll work with a clear sense of direction, and b) you'll be able to finish the session knowing that you've done enough for the day. In my experience, writers who work without this task specification often "dawdle" aimlessly (e.g., they keep reworking an introduction beyond the point of diminishing returns). Equally important, the same writers often feel that unless an entire manuscript is finished, they haven't done enough. No wonder, then, that writing without breaking the task into specifiable units can overwhelm writers.

7. Keep daily charts. Graph at least three things: a) time spent writing, b) page equivalents finished, and c) percent of planned task completed. Use the charts as a prod to activity, as feedback about the effectiveness of your stimulus control procedures, as feedback about the practicality of your daily goals, and as a visible reward for working. These charts work best, in my experience, when displayed publicly.

8. Plan beyond daily goals. Schedule the stages of a manuscript in terms of weeks, again with specifiable and measurable goals so that you'll feel clear about where you're headed and about knowing when you've done enough. As plans grow larger, they necessarily involve more uncertainty; you'll need to proceed, sometimes, before achieving closure and comfort about whether you'll meet the schedule. If anything, experience will probably show you that you're allotting too much time for preliminary stages. It is often best to put limits on generative stages (e.g., working with a conceptual outline produced in one session whether you feel ready or not) and on rough drafts.

9. Share your writing with supportive, constructive friends before you feel ready to go public. If other readers know that they're being asked to appraise writing in its formative stages, they'll feel less judgmental and more inclined to offer advice for changes. If, in contrast, they're asked to read a finished draft, they may suspect

that you don't really want to make substantial changes. To get beyond the vague comments typically produced by friends (e.g., "interesting"), give your reader specific questions, especially about parts of the paper you suspect need improvement. Going public with your formative work accelerates and improves most writing.

10. Try to work on two or three writing projects concurrently. Alternatives reduce the tedium that can emerge in working on the same project too regularly. Often, the alternative projects produce cross-fertilization of ideas.

A final caution: Each of the seventeen points just covered is critical to ensure writing; they merit rereading, especially as reminders once you're under way. In my experience, many writers, once they establish some momentum, are tempted to abandon many of these rules. The point of establishing and maintaining these rules as lasting habits may not be apparent when writing is easy. But without these habits in reserve, you'll probably stop writing when real distractions and discouragements resurface.

Dealing with Objections to Environmental/External Controls

We've already seen some hints of objections to stimulus control of writing. (You may have felt some.) Most people would prefer to write with the sole aid of internal, intrinsic motivation.

And many people, in my experience, wonder if stimulus control can work for them. A typical comment: "I wouldn't follow the rules. I'd cheat." In fact, few people do. The main reason, as far as I can tell, is deceptively simple. Rearranging one's writing environment and habits tends to make writing a more probable event. Once writing becomes regular, its occurrence becomes as habitual as other recurrent activities such as teeth brushing. We could cheat in regard to brushing our teeth, but we rarely do. We rarely even think about it.

But even where people can see the merit of that argument for stimulus control, they may hang onto the other reservation. They still suppose that "forced" writing will feel unnatural and contrived and that the writing would necessarily lack qualities like creativity. I encounter this objection so commonly that I devote a regular part of my research on writing to it. One such study is abstracted here.

Does Stimulus Control of Writing Impede Creativity?

The test was relatively simple.[2] I gathered 27 faculty members from universities as volunteer research subjects. All complained of difficulties in completing writing projects; all evidenced uncompleted projects that could be finished. Each met with me briefly once a week to provide charts of their writing activities and to share their logs of creative ideas for writing experienced during the previous week.

All 27 faculty filled out a daily "thought-list" sheet headed with clear instructions (e.g., "Do not enter ideas that have already been listed") during each time when writing was scheduled. But not all 27 actually wrote anything beyond their log entries. Nine subjects agreed to put off all but emergency writing for 10 weeks. They complied eagerly with the abstinence program while supposing, as a rule, that planned abstinence from writing would engender a lot of useful, creative ideas for writing.

Another nine subjects scheduled the same 50 writing sessions, but were encouraged to write only when in the mood. These spontaneous subjects began, as did the abstinent subjects, by supposing their condition was favorable to the production of creativity.

The third group of nine subjects agreed to a contingency management plan that forced them to write during nearly all of the 50 scheduled sessions. To ensure regular writing, they used a highly expensive contingency; a prewritten check would have been sent to a hated organization on any day they didn't produce three page equivalents of writing. These contingency subjects began somewhat glumly, certain they would produce writing, but dubious about its creativity.

The expensive contingency did, of course, produce verifiably regular writing. And, not surprisingly, the spontaneous and abstinent groups produced less:

Output of Typed Equivalent Pages and Creative Ideas Produced Per Scheduled/Potential Writing Day

Group (writing condition)	$\overline{X}$ Number Pages	Modal Number of Days Between Creative Ideas
Contingency Management (forced)	3.2	1
Spontaneous	0.9	2
Abstinent	0.2	5

The more important result concerned productivity of creative ideas for writing. The abstinent group listed creative thoughts at a rate of about one per week. Spontaneous subjects produced creative ideas sporadically, much as they produced writing, at a rate of about one idea every other day. Contingent subjects, finally, produced the highest and most stable outputs of creativity, at levels consistently above a useful, novel idea per writing day. Contingent subjects also produced far and away the most spontaneous reports of enjoying their writing.

This recorded response typifies comments made by the "forced" writers:

- "It really isn't what I thought it would be. I don't feel the pressure because I don't even think about it very often. As a matter of fact, if I did think about it, I'd realize that I'm the one who agreed to follow the plan. I should get the credit, or at least some of it. It feels good to be so self-disciplined. What I really like, though, is how easy it is to start writing. No struggle. I look forward to it. I think about what I'm going to write during the day. Sometimes I'm tempted to start sooner. That sure doesn't sound like me." [laughs]

Why should forced, regular writing facilitate creative thinking? In part, evidently, because it encourages regular thinking about writing. One thing that characterizes successful writers is their daily preoccupation with writing.[6] They enjoy thinking about their writing. Problem writers, conversely, spend little time thinking about writing;[7] only rarely do they develop much sense of momentum or continuity in their writing.

Another reason derives from the real nature of creativity. Writing, like other creative and complex skills, must be practiced regularly for good effect. Writing, like other "arts," involves the hard work of careful, detailed observation. And, writing practiced habitually can produce the other essential ingredients of creativity: the elaboration of thinking processes such as "directed remembering" and a "readiness to perceive the unexpected."[8]

In sum, then:

1. External contingencies that "force" writers to write regularly seem to facilitate, not impede, creativity.

2. Spontaneity in writing is ineffective, compared to contingency management, for producing written copy or novel and useful ideas in the long run.

Is Contingency Management the Critical Ensurer?

Having seen the evidence for the efficacy of contingency management in producing both quantity and quality of writing, many writers remain uncomfortable. Some ask how I know that it's the contingency management (and not something else like a changed attitude) that accounts for the productivity?

One way to demonstrate the critical role of contingency management in productivity is to systematically add and subtract the contingency for daily writing. The result for the vast majority of blocked writers with whom I've worked looks like the graph of this individual writer shown in Figure 3 below:

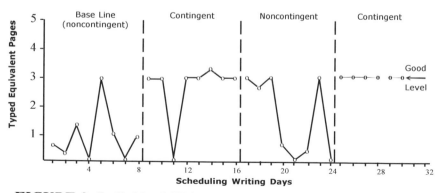

FIGURE 3. Individual Writer Performance.

During the first segment of the writing program (non-contingent), the previously blocked writer met regularly with me and received advice about writing and got training in spontaneous/generative writing. Writing occurred when the writer felt like writing; during this "base line" phase, writing was technically non-contingent.

During the second phase (contingent), the priority principle was used to ensure regular writing. In this case, a mild contingency like earning access to a daily shower was used to bring daily writing productivity to a stable level of four pages a day. It eventually worked, as mild contingencies typically do.

By the end of the second phase, though, this writer shared a feeling almost universal to having success with contingency management—a certainty that the contingency was no longer necessary. Most people, in my experience, feel confident then that they can write regularly on their own, using their newly strengthened intrinsic motivation.

The third phase of the graph (a return to non-contingent conditions) shows what almost always happens when formerly blocked writers work without the external contingency. Writing becomes irregular. Feelings of blocking reemerge.

When, in the fourth phase (a return to contingent conditions), writing was again "forced" by external pressures, this writer expressed the feeling common at this point relief. Writing output stabilized and the writer reported greater confidence and satisfaction in writing than during non-contingent phases. At follow-up periods of six months and one year, this writer, like most who completed such a program, continued to use external contingencies "to create discipline," to chart, and to produce regular amounts of writing.

Are There Alternatives to Contingency Management?

Presenting these data may convince people that contingency management works, but it still may not make them feel like writing. They may feel like the person holding the picture of the woman who found success by writing during cab rides: "If that's what it takes, forget it!"

So I reassure writers with reminders of the advantages of the results-first approach. I re-review the claims of satisfaction made by writers working under contingent conditions. And, then, I mention alternatives to contingency management: Contingency management remains necessary only so long as writers do not make the occurrence of daily writing habitual by other means–e.g., by rearranging their daily priorities and their writing environments. When, in my experience, writers make writing a realistic priority in daily living, and when they arrange writing locations to minimize distractions, then external contingencies can be superfluous.

But even these experienced writers continue to value contingency management. They recall its effectiveness in helping make writing habitual. And they realize its potential importance during disruptive, troubled periods.

Another hint about alternatives is that simple contingency management and other stimulus control techniques comprise only the second of four essential stages in dealing with the dynamics of writing problems:

1. *Automaticity*, or establishing momentum, can be effected via techniques such as spontaneous and generative writing.
2. *Stimulus control* techniques help ensure regular writing by making writing a non-distracted, habitual activity.
3. *Self-control* of writing can be achieved via practices including the observation and modification of the inner discourse (i.e., self-talk) connected with writing.
4. *Social skills* of writing include making one's writing more public and more publicly supported. Done properly, writing becomes more a public than a private act.

This list, of course, gets us a bit ahead of the story. We will deal with self-control and social skills in the next chapter. For now, this list illustrates prospects of relying on more than external controls for effective unblocking.

Perhaps you've noticed something else. I've meandered for an unusually long time before settling into the actual exercise of "forcing" writing. Experience, some of it disheartening, has been my guide; this is the point at which writers are most hesitant, most likely to quit; this is the point at which I feel the need to provide the clearest rationales for my advice.

Experiencing the Priority Principle

My advice: Begin with the most hard-hearted, surefire form of the priority principle, contingency management. It works.

Contingency Management

Find times when you can write each weekday for at least 30 minutes (but generally for no longer than 1-2 hours). Ensure your working presence at these prescheduled sessions in two ways. First, make out a chart/graph for the week ahead by pre-listing the dates and times when you'll write. Enter the times actually worked, even zeroes for days when you don't work, each day at the end of the scheduled writing time.

Then, establish a contingency for daily writing. Make a valued daily activity (e.g., newspaper reading, television watching, showering . . . even housecleaning) contingent on completing a scheduled writing period first. Some recurrent activities such as eating make poor contingencies because going without them may be unhealthy. (If you're trying to diet, having a meal as the reward for writing builds in too convenient an excuse for not writing.)

Many people need to experiment with contingencies until they find one that works reliably. If, for example, you find that you can go without showers rather than write regularly, you may need a different, possibly even a more expensive contingency. Or, in contrast, you may find that the contingency you've chosen is somehow inappropriate and that something else better suits your needs. I knew a student, for instance, whose idea for a punishment for not writing was sleeping without her pillow; she eventually found something that was less problematic. Sleeping without a pillow can be like earning forgiveness for one's misbehavior. But the prospect of, for example, allowing one's money to be sent to a despised organization induces real and effective guilt.

You'll have to see what works most reasonably and reliably for you. And, you'll need to use good sense. Writing made too high a priority—so that it excludes a social life or proper attention to teaching is doomed to failure.

Once you've settled into a comfortable, regular regimen of writing, move beyond the requirement of putting in a minimum of time per daily session. Add specific, realistic requirements for a) minimal levels of written output (e.g., in a 30-minute session, aim for a goal of one typed-equivalent page) and b) add sub-goals to be met in each writing session (e.g., a completed revision of a conceptual outline; a revised first page of a rough draft). Requiring a minimal level of daily output helps to move you out of "dawdling" strategies that delay writing. Requiring completion of a specified sub-goal in the overall project does something similar; it helps propel writers toward longer term goals.

Here, perhaps more than anywhere, you'll need to experiment. You'll need to find comfortable but challenging levels of output to set as minimums. You'll need to formulate ways of counting activities such as outlining or revision in terms of page equivalents. And, most important, you'll need to plan the entire course of completing a writing project so that you can make meaningful decisions about how much or how little to plan for each daily session. With a little practice, this sort of planning isn't difficult or even very time-consuming.

Stimulus Control

Once you're working regularly, you'll develop a better sense of what distracts and disrupts your writing. Recheck the 17 guidelines for rearranging writing environments and writing habits listed earlier in this chapter. Make adjustments accordingly.

In my experience, many writers do not see the real value of arranging quietude for writing, of writing with another writer, of working on several projects simultaneously, etc., until they write regularly. But, then, that's how the results-first approach typically works.

Time Management

Books on time management abound. The classic is Lakein's bestseller, *How to Get Control of Your Time and Your Life.*[9] It, like many such books, may seem to promise too much. But its admonitions can work. Lakein advises making long-range statements of goals, categorizing goals and tasks in a system of priorities, breaking jobs into smaller components, and scheduling work time.

We, as you doubtless noticed, have already been discussing some time management procedures.

What constitutes effective time management includes formal planning with regular adjustments. Once your writing regimen is under way, you might profit by charting your daily expenditure of time in 30-minute blocks. You'll need to see, with the aid of experimentation, where you're over investing or wasting time. You'll need to see where you can work in regular times for high priority activities such as social life and exercising. Then, perhaps, comes writing. And, most critical, you'll need to work out clear statements of your goals in writing, working, socializing, etc.

Done properly and patiently, time management of writing activities can positively affect your other daily activities. It should make life feel less harried.

Not surprisingly, though, the idea of carrying out such revisions in daily scheduling, even if they occur gradually, can seem threatening. Some writers at this stage feel anxious about giving up too much control. One person at a recent workshop of mine suddenly exclaimed:

"My God, you're asking us to change our whole lifestyles!"

She was right. But I reminded her of two important considerations: She would decide on the changes. And, if she did resort to planning and time management, she would probably be more in control of her life than before.

Limit-Setting

Effective time management includes one more factor, limit-setting. Many writers I've worked with excel in setting up stimulus control procedures and time-managed schedules for writing except in one dimension: They persevere too long in one or more of the stages of writing. They may spend too much time preparing notes from the literature relevant to their project, they may revise formal drafts too many times. You probably know what I mean.

Limit-setting means just what it says; you set limits on time investments so that you will work more efficiently during sessions and so that you will have "permission" to move to the next phase of writing in timely fashion. Restated in terms of already familiar concepts, limit-setting means learning to . . .

1. *Start* writing before you may feel you're ready.

2. *Finish* writing before you may feel you're ready.

3. *Know* when you've done enough with your writing project.

Knowing when you've done enough or that you can begin without over-preparation is a critical skill in writing efficiently and painlessly. Without this kind of knowing, writing problems loom at the ready. Without limit-setting, professors expose themselves to an especially insidious kind of stress–of never being able to leave campus feeling they've done enough.[10]

The problem with mastering limit-setting, in my experience, is that you must learn much of it on your own, via trial and error. Its workable formulas vary across individuals. But if you can, you'll master one of the critical deterrents to overcoming both perfectionistic and procrastinating styles of behaving.

The person who can begin something, including writing, without having to be perfectly prepared, in fact takes pressure off him- or herself. Ditto for giving up some control over perfectionism by leaving a project with imperfections in the hands of peer reviewers. Both tactics teach the values of giving up one kind of control (i.e., wanting to be perfect) for another, healthier kind of control (i.e., being able to work and communicate comfortably, without unnecessary anxiety).

Similarly, the person who exercises the planfulness of stimulus control techniques and time management overcomes procrastination. Indeed, planfulness is the opposite of procrastination. With activities scheduled in terms of workable sub-goals and of reordered priorities, writing will occur as regularly, as painlessly as other important and recurrent things. Because, finally, this planfulness specifies the amount to be done each day, writers know when they've done enough. This daily sense of completion removes one of the best excuses to procrastinate–the overwhelming feeling that one can never do enough to complete a writing project and, so, is better off doing it at the last minute.

Consider this: procrastination offers the only form of limit-setting obvious to many writers. It may be better, they suppose, to limit themselves to a few frantic days of working under the gun than allowing themselves to spend nearly all their time writing over weeks, even months.

What these procrastinating writers ignore, though, are the aversive properties associated with last-minute writing–fatigue, anxiety, lack of confidence about writing ability, among them. These writers also ignore the realities of planful, managed writing. Most scholarly writing can be done with small, daily investments of time, regardless of academic specialty.

Individualized Programs

I have already hinted at two individualized programs: Procrastinators and perfectionists are especially in need of planful, enforced writing. They are also most resistant, in my experience, to trying them. Both types of resistance seem to revolve around issues of control.

Perfectionists, perhaps out of some insecurity about being discovered as incompetents, have difficulty "letting go." They dislike beginning until they feel fully prepared. They abhor finishing until their obsessions about imperfections and overlooked sources, etc., are quelled. Even while admitting how long these perfectionistic tendencies can delay writing without real justification, perfectionists are understandably uncomfortable with strategies like "writing before you're ready."

Perfectionists, as much as procrastinators, need powerful incentives to try planful but limited writing. I often advise strong forms of contingency management for both.

Procrastinators, I've learned, carry deep philosophical objections to planfulness. They enjoy joking about their poor work habits; they sometimes reveal suspicions that disciplined, efficient people should be uniformed as Storm Troopers. Worse yet, in their ambivalence about overcoming procrastination, procrastinators often seek help and then find clever ways to reject it. They particularly resent feeling controlled. And, they don't like others to discover the inefficiency that lies hidden under their displays of busyness.

What works best with procrastinators, in my experience, is presenting the system to them, coaxing them to sample it, and then letting them decide when to employ it. Once procrastinators make the decision, their stubbornness and busyness can turn into virtues.

Impatience, another diagnostic category, deserves special mention here. Impatient writers want to finish their projects quickly; they express real discomfort with a plan in which they produce only a page or two a day. They (much like many of the obese patients I've seen in my role as a clinical psychologist) want quick and substantial results. Impatient writers need to be coached to try a method that, deep down, they recognize as slow- but-sure. Contingency management, again, ensures both daily participation and almost certain success in the long run.

Other Writers, in my experience, need stimulus control and time management techniques only until (and unless) they prove to be reliably productive without them. Few do.

Notes

[1]Wallace, I. (1971). *The writing of one novel*. New York: Simon & Schuster.

[2]Boice, R. (1984). Contingency management in writing and the appearance of creative ideas: Implications for the treatment of writing blocks. *Behaviour Research & Therapy, 21*, 537-543.

[3]Nemy, E. (1982). Doing it all: The people who work and write. *New York Times*, September 24, A24.

[4]Nurnberger, J.T., & Zimmerman, J. (1970). Applied analysis of human behavior. *Behavior Therapy, 1*, 59-69.

[5]Hall, B.L., & Hursch, D.E. (1982). An evaluation of the effects of a time management training program on work efficiency. *Journal of Organizational Behavior Management, 3*, 73-96.

[6]Gould, J.D. (1980). Experiments in composing letters. In L.W. Gregg & E.R. Steinberg (Eds.), *Cognitive processes in writing*. Erlbaum: Hillsdale, NJ.

[7]Perl, S. (1980). *Five writers writing: Case studies of the composing process of unskilled college writers*. Dissertation, New York University.

[8]Perkins, D.N. (1981). *The mind's best work*. Cambridge, MA: Harvard University Press.

[9]Lakein, A. (1973). *How to get control of your time and your life*. New York: The New American Library.

[10]Boice, R., & Myers, P.E. (1987). Which setting is healthier and happier, academe or private practice? *Professional Psychology: Research and Practice, 18*, 526-529.

Chapter Seven

The Four-Step Plan

"Learn to write well, or not to write at all."

THE QUOTE comes from John Dryden, a seventeenth century poet. It demonstrates how long writers have been following bad advice. Writing experts still give similar advice; they help provide the discouraged and/or perfectionistic writers I work with.

Dryden might have been more constructive with advice like this:

"Learn to write happily and to an appreciative audience, or not at all."

Even then I wonder about the "or not at all" part.

I generally mention my revision of Dryden's advice, about the value of appreciating writing and being appreciated as a writer, during this stage of writing programs and workshops. By now, most of the professors with whom I have worked are established as regimented and productive writers.

Why now, when things seem to be going well? Why not leave well enough alone? Because, I've learned, externally imposed discipline may not be enough for writers. If writing doesn't become intrinsically and socially rewarding, writers tend to burn out.

Origins of the Four-Step Plan

I didn't always get this far. Until recently, my sense of responsibility to troubled writers expired once their writing was regular for at least a year. I hurried on to the ever-growing waiting list of colleagues who felt unable to write.

I assumed that intrinsic and social rewards would take care of themselves, once writing was regular; that was, after all, what had apparently happened to me.

Fortunately, many of my former "graduates" of writing programs continued to keep charts which they shared with me annually. I noticed a curious pattern in the casual conversations accompanying these reports: while they evidenced continued success in dimensions like productivity and publication, most expressed a regret like this one:

- "I don't mean to sound ungrateful. You've been very helpful and I've gotten more writing done than I had hoped. But I still don't like writing. I still have to wrestle myself down to my desk to get started. Sometimes I remain nauseous all the way through a writing session. I had hoped that writing would be like jogging, that the pain would be temporary and that I would miss it if I skipped a day. But I don't [laughs]. What I'd like to know, I guess, is when it gets better. If it doesn't, if it can't, then I can't see continuing to torment myself like this, day after day."

I was surprised, but only momentarily. I had just begun collecting evidence about the cognitive changes that accompany writing block therapies and, to an extent, this series of studies confirmed my original expectations.[1] For example, blocked and unblocked writers talk to themselves about writing in predictably different ways:

Type of Self-Talk Reported

	maladaptive	neutral	psych-up
Blockers (N=40)	74%	19%	7%
Nonblockers (N=20)	42%	9%	49%

There was no surprise in learning that blockers reported telling themselves 10 times as many negative as positive things about writing.

What did surprise me, though, was the relatively high level of negativism in the thinking of nonblockers. Why did these people, who evidenced no history of overt blocking, engage in so much of the kinds of inner discourse that could make writing more difficult?

Further analysis provided part of the answer. When the thousands of thought-list cards were separated into categories of blocking cognitions (e.g., fear of evaluation), an unexpected category dominated for both blockers and nonblockers–an aversion to the fatigue and unpleasantness of the act of writing:

Percentage of All Negative Self-Talk Devoted to Dislike for the Act of Writing

Blockers (N=40)	33%
Nonblockers (N=20)	25%

In other words, productivity and success in publishing as a writer provide little assurance that writing becomes a welcome, enjoyable activity. Many of these writers, whether blocked or productive, seemed to loathe the act of writing.

Writing programs must, it seemed to me, offer more than the promise of being able to work but with little comfort.

Another part of the answer came later, in follow-up work with the 40 writers who had been blocked and unable to write. I asked them why, despite writing regularly, they still reported such loathing. Part of their discomfort, they said, owed to the hard work of writing. "It's like speaking to a man who's nearly deaf," one said. "You must be so damned careful to be clear that you get tired."

But the bigger part of their discomfort was more psychological. In essence, they reported frustration over three disappointments with their ostensible successes in writing: a) they didn't yet feel intrinsically motivated or rewarded regarding writing; b) they resented the usually unsupportive, sometimes rude style of the "gatekeepers" to publishing such as reviewers and editors;[2] and c) they wondered, after all their hard work, if anyone would appreciate what they were trying to communicate.

At last, feeling a bit foolish at not having seen it before, I realized that writing programs should be extended to include two more steps. Adaptive solutions to writing problems, I decided, should include reliable ways of establishing *momentum, disciplined productivity, intrin-*

sic motivation, and *satisfaction*. I began a "recall program" whereby former graduates were encouraged to come back for post-graduate work.

The Four Steps

Two of the four steps toward writing without blocking are already familiar: establishing momentum via techniques such as spontaneous and generative writing, and establishing regular productivity via stimulus control techniques. For the sake of making them memorable, I've relabeled those first steps as . . .
1. *automaticity*
2. *externality*

The third and fourth steps follow from what I've just said about intrinsic and social motivation. They, too, are relabeled as . . .
3. *self-control*
4. *sociality*

Each of the four steps, even the already familiar, merits explanation in terms of an integrated, holistic approach to unblocking.

Automaticity

Automaticity in writing comes via unself-conscious methods such as spontaneous and generative writing. Automaticity releases your inner writer.[3] It also (as we have already seen) establishes momentum, bypasses internal censors, generates rhythm and voice, and builds confidence in abilities to be spontaneous, playful, and creative.

Automaticity is obviously important to the writer who feels stuck. But, it acts in even more valuable ways, once writing is under way, by providing access to spontaneous sources of image and proportion. Successful, joyful writing demands constant shifts between the rational, planful mind and the calm, resourceful spontaneous mind. Balance is everything . . . well, almost.

Externality

Externality means external controls that ensure writing. External controls, as we experienced earlier, work in a variety of ways to increase the likelihood of writing; used in strong form, they virtually guarantee writing.

The priority principle, for example, makes writing a higher priority by requiring its practice before moving on to more desirable, recurrent activities. Related forms of stimulus control include arranging settings and schedules that make writing a higher probability behavior–sometimes by limiting alternatives to writing, sometimes by making rewards or punishments contingent on its occurrence or nonoccurrence.

Stimulus control methods, including time management, work externally by rearranging the writer's environment and schedule. They help writers work regularly, productively, and even creatively. To an extent, external controls can help with psychological aspects of writing: Externality, like automaticity, builds confidence. It brings a sense of discipline to writing. It shows that usual complaints about too little time for writing are invariably incorrect. And, external controls can help clarify goals and priorities of writing.

Self-Control

Self-control has many meanings. Some people use it to mean the kind of access to mechanisms that induce voluntary control over autonomic functions such as heart rate.[4] Others label a person as self-controlled when he or she sets up external control techniques that ensure planned behaviors.[5] Still others equate self-control with strong willpower.[6]

I agree that all three pertain to psychological well-being. But, I contend that the kind of self-control most pertinent to writing resides with the source of the self the rational consciousness. Earlier (Chapter 5), we reviewed ways in which the conscious mind helps writers: it carries on narratives, it assigns causes, it encourages an awareness of time, and it builds a sense of who it is that "stars" in all these narratives–the self. Consciousness operates, in large part, by means of inner conversations and directives.

When you consider what self-talk can do (e.g., it affects moods, judges self-worth, anticipates performance problems), you won't be surprised at its roles in writing problems. As the negativism of self-talk gets far out of control, overt problems such as blocking (e.g., an inability to start) occur. When some writers escalate mere fears into debilitating panic, they tell themselves a) how poorly they will perform compared to others, b) how embarrassed they will be if their efforts are rejected, c) how unreasonable the assignment is, etc.[7] Writers can literally talk themselves into blocking.

Self-talk under only partial control seems to be the culprit in what I call subtle or covert blocking. Writers write but only under the duress of reminders about how fatiguing and unrewarding the work will be. They can do it, but they can't stop loathing it.

Control over one's consciousness, especially over its tendencies to distortion and negativism, is what I define as self-control. The locus of this control is easily specified–in self-talk. The results of establishing control of self-talk include intrinsic motivation and intrinsic satisfaction for writing. More planful use of inner discourse can help generate positive moods, enthusiasm for writing, and confidence that practical steps are under way to produce writing that will be well-organized and well-received.

Cognitive self-control of writing is a demanding but manageable task for almost all writers with whom I've worked. Why, then, isn't it more widely used to help problem writers?

The answer is not inaccessibility or inexperience; we already "know" about cognitive self-therapies.[8] We can talk ourselves out of an angry mood and irrational thoughts; consider a situation where you recognize the problem as a traffic jam, one over which you have no control. You have probably learned ways to talk yourself "down" in such situations. You can even, perhaps, coach yourself past many of the performance anxieties that accompany most writing problems. You may know that saying, "If I just get started, I won't feel so anxious," helps as you plunge into spontaneous writing.

The problem is that too few of us take the process far enough to get rid of the discomfort and loathing. Why? For one thing, few of us have been encouraged to reflect much about the act of writing. Instead, we've been led to believe that writing is a special, mysterious process and that writers work best by sticking to a spontaneous style. For another thing, few people pay much attention to their self-talk unless it becomes overwhelmingly intrusive. Generally, we let it chatter on, even when it says bad things, ruins our fun, and keeps us in a bad mood.

Research in cognitive therapy,[9] including my own, suggests this step-wise format for establishing more adaptive patterns of self-talk:

   First phase: Self-monitoring–Much of what we say to ourselves goes unobserved. Good thing, considering that much of it is nothing but the boring narrative account of what is happening or of what we should be doing. Some things that we do, like driving on a freeway, are too mundane to even require self-talk. During those times, we stop being conscious. Some things, like drawing or spontaneous writing, really don't work well until we inhibit conscious processes. So, for much of the time, self- talk may be insignificant or else nonexistent.

Usually, then, self-observation is unproductive or impossible. Self-observation is important when we notice we are feeling uncomfortable. Bad moods are usually accompanied by negative self-talk.

When I ask writers to report their self-talk at these times, they typically resist. Some claim, initially at least, that they can't remember what they were saying to themselves. Others simply admit their discomfort in discovering how negative, even bizarre, their self-talk can be.

They learn, however, that observing self-talk can be fascinating and useful. They discover surprising regularities; negative self-talk usually runs in repetitive scripts. And, they find themselves worrying about improbable things, exaggerating potentially bad outcomes, and convincing themselves that they are inadequate, indecent people. When they, figuratively, stand back and observe those negative scripts, they appreciate what helps make writing unnecessarily difficult and discomforting. They are, in my experience, amazed to discover what has been going on inside their brains. And they are motivated to do something about it.

One approach to developing skills in observing self-talk resembles the method used by people learning to keep dream diaries:

1. Begin by assuming that negative self-talk exists, especially during anxious or depressed moods, even if its presence is not immediately apparent. If you must, make a start by writing down your best guess of your negative self-talk. (Later, when you gain better access to your self-talk, you may be surprised at how closely your guesses resemble the typical scripts of your negative inner discourse.)

2. Work at observing ongoing inner discourse. But don't try to rush the process. Observation works best when carried out in unhurried, unobtrusive fashion. Plan to react to observations of disturbing self-talk in detached, objective fashion. When you notice yourself saying something absurd, simply make a calm, detached re-

mark like this: "Oh, isn't that interesting, there goes another weird thought."

3. Learn to categorize your self-talk into categories like adaptiveness and maladaptiveness. For example, most worrisome self-talk, upon closer scrutiny, can be seen to be unnecessary and unproductive. One way to help judge maladaptiveness of self-talk is to observe its accompanying mood state. Inner discourse that focuses on themes like victimization or anticipated failures is rarely accompanied by positive affect.

4. Work at identifying functions of maladaptive self-talk; i.e., do the scripts provide secondary gains like protecting you from failure by encouraging you to avoid maximal involvement in a task? Recognize, where appropriate, that some scripts may be nothing more than ingrained old habits with little remaining function. Habitual scripts, in my experience, play a major role in maintaining the loathing for writing that hounds even productive and successful writers.

One more thing can help: The formal assessments in the appendices include one questionnaire specifically designed to diagnose cognitive tendencies to blocking. Your scores on the Checklist for Cognitions/Emotions in Blocking (CCB) can provide useful information in ways including an overall index of maladaptive self-talk connected to writing and specific indications where self-talk contributes to syndromes such as impatience or dysphoria.

As you undertake these analyses of your self-talk, comparisons with other writers may be useful. My own research with a sample of 60 writers (40 of whom were blocked) produced this characterization of maladaptive cognitions:[1]

Type of Blocking Cognition	Blockers (N=40)	Nonblockers (N=20)
	Numbers indicate $\overline{X}$ frequency per subject	
1. "Writing is too fatiguing, unpleasant"	26.0	16.6
2. "It's O.K. to procrastinate"	11.5	3.8
3. "I'm too dysphoric, depressed, upset to write"	8.3	2.0

| | Blockers (N=40) | Nonblockers (N=20) |
Type of Blocking Cognition	Numbers indicate $\bar{X}$ frequency per subject	
4. "I feel impatient about writing"	8.0	4.5
5. "Writing should be mistake-free and superior"	5.2	1.1
6. "Writing will lead to negative evaluations"	2.9	0.7
7. "Good writing must follow rules"	0.5	0.4

Being able to categorize negative self-talk about writing in terms of category as well as function (e.g., where you talk yourself into procrastinating because beginning earlier will mean having to face fears of humiliation sooner) is critical to the next phase of establishing self-control over blocking.

Second phase: Thought-stopping–Merely recognizing maladaptive thoughts sometimes disarms and disrupts them. Generally, though, more active measures are necessary.

Thought-stopping can be as simple as issuing a command to oneself like this: Stop! Some people, caught up in obsessive patterns of thought, even carry a card that says STOP! with them; upon recognizing the offending self-talk, they pull out the card and heed the command. It sounds silly, but it works.

When such simple procedures fail, thought-stopping requires a bit more effort and planning. The most important component follows from the advice given about observing; try to analyze the self-talk from a detached, objective vantage. That is, consider what you're saying as though an impartial jury were listening. Then, consider the adaptiveness of your self-talk through the eyes of that imaginary jury. Would they rate your inner discourse as realistic, as helpful? Would they conclude that you're being too pessimistic, too self-critical, too emotional and subjective? Would they notice, for example, that in your self-talk, you tend to confuse statements with facts? Are, for example, reviewers' opinions accepted as incontestable facts–and then, for good measure, elaborated into devastatingly negative messages?

The more habitual and patterned the self-talk, the more difficult it may be to stop or to remain stopped. Some of the most vicious scripts sneak back into inner discourse almost immediately. When that happens, and it often does, then the third phase of cognitive therapy helps.

Third phase: Thought-substitution–In general, negative self-talk is easier to supplant than to stop. Trying to think about nothing, as we all know, is difficult. But planning to replace negative cognitions with more upbeat, constructive self-talk can help fill that void in adaptive fashion.

Indirect evidence already presented indicates the potential usefulness of thought-substitution for blocked writers; blocked writers were seven times more likely to engage in "psych-up" self-talk than were unblocked writers. Ongoing research suggests, moreover, that thought-substitution techniques help foster unblocking in two ways: they can help accelerate the initial unblocking process in a minority of writers. And, they do seem to be pivotal in ridding already productive writers of their loathsome self-talk connected to writing.

The procedure for thought-substitution revolves around two simple concepts: *planfulness* and *rehearsal*. Planfulness begins with recollections of negativistic scripts and the generation of more positive, helpful scripts to replace them. Where, for example, self-talk usually focuses on the tiresomeness of writing, the theme might better emphasize the feelings of relief and satisfaction that await the end of the writing session. Similarly, self-talk focusing on the likelihood of a rudely critical response from reviewers might better concern the realistic aspects of reviewing–that reviewers carry out a largely thankless, difficult task, that they often do provide help, and that they rarely act to victimize you for personal reasons.[9] You can decide, then, to concentrate on intrinsically satisfying reasons to write and on the prospects of getting your work published eventually. Be able to remind yourself that many classic novels, scientific articles, etc., were initially rejected, often emphatically. Reviewers' opinions are just that, opinions.

When you've crafted new scripts to replace the negative self-talk, rehearse them. Without careful preparation in role-playing and refining the new scripts, the old scripts will be difficult to supplant. One good way to rehearse: write out the old scripts and the new scripts and revise the new ones until they are clear winners in an imaginary debate.

Then, role-play a scenario where you feel negatively about writing, conjure up the old script until it has momentum, and try substituting the new script for self-talk. Rehearsals, when carried out patiently and reflectively, produce several advantages: like stage rehearsals, they point out areas where the dialog is too artificial and unconvincing; they build confidence, and they help make the dialog automatic. Until new scripts become somewhat automatic or reflexive, they cannot supplant old scripts reliably.

Fourth phase: Self-rewards–Many writers who master the first three phases of cognitive modification struggle with the fourth phase. They prefer to dismiss their success in establishing cognitive self-control as something that was overdue and, therefore, not very meritorious.

But self-congratulations are critical to self-control. Awareness of improvement and of your role in effecting it brings self-confidence and builds intrinsic motivation to continue working at improvement. Self-reward requires little more than a verbal pat-on-the-back.

Self-control that emphasizes self-reward does more than build confidence and intrinsic motivation, according to my ongoing research. It also helps make writing a painless, enjoyable task–nearly as painless and enjoyable as good conversation.

Self-controlled writing even brings paradoxical change: It acts to help change writing into a less private act. Self-controlled writers, in my experience, reach out to make their writing more public, more sociable, more socially appreciated. Their own positiveness probably even elicits more positiveness in readers.

Sociality

Most writing is, after all, a social act. Strange, then, that we typically do most of it in private, without discussing the process with others. No wonder that writers tend to feel lonely and unappreciated. No wonder they struggle to find what composition teachers call a sense of audience. No wonder, with so great a reliance on reclusiveness, that writers fall prey to anxiety, depression, suspiciousness, and blocking.

The solution to these usual patterns of social isolation is no different than with any other form of "social skills deficits:" it focuses on helping writers become more socially skilled.[10] The program of social skills I have developed with writers has four basic components:

Soliciting comments/criticism on writing across stages–One way to make writing more sociable is to share it with various people as you develop it. In my experience, many other writers welcome requests to look at writing in its formative stages, especially in abstract versions like conceptual outlines.

Given this stimulus, other writers reciprocate by sharing their formative work. At the least, writing proceeds with more social input; as a rule, exchanges of this sort produce enjoyable exchanges of ideas. Sometimes, shared writing leads to chances for collaborative writing.

Experience has taught me to impress these cautions on writers who are about to solicit comments/criticism: First, structure part of your request for specific feedback so that readers will respond to meaningful questions about how well the paper accomplishes the purposes you have in mind. Otherwise, you'll have no one but yourself to blame if your informal critics tend to the usual extremes–i.e., either vague compliments or torrents of picayune criticism.

Second, use several critics, particularly a person whom you suspect will disapprove. You won't learn much by relying solely on critics who share your biases. Furthermore, don't suppose that you're imposing; most writers see such requests for help as a compliment; most, once moved out of their passivity and reclusiveness, enjoy talking about writing.

Third, add another, protective form of structure to your requests for feedback. Subtly ask critics to begin and end their remarks with specific, positive comments about your writing. You won't need to explain this request; writers immediately recognize its merit (and how much they would enjoy receiving criticism in a similar format).

Prepare for negative criticism–Resist self-talk that casts you as a chronic, helpless victim. Prepare self-talk that defuses criticism (e.g., "I don't think I agree with it, but perhaps I can salvage something useful from it; perhaps I need to consider the possibility that something unintentional in my writing would elicit similar reactions in other readers").

Then, do the improbable. Try to respond to your critic with calm agreement. You can almost always find something in the criticism that is conceivably correct, at least from the critic's perspective. Then, ask for more criticism! At the least, this ploy defuses the usual emotionality of critical exchanges. The critic discovers that you've listened (in part, because you've reflected his/her criticism in your statement of agreement), that you're not angry, and that you hope to learn from him or her.

Asking for additional information often helps win the critic over as a real supporter. Critics tend to respond with reassurance and compliments and with more constructive criticisms.

As you learn to respond to criticisms in this socially skilled fashion, you help make writing a less stressful experience. Moreover, you'll enlist critics who welcome your requests for help.

Build social networks–Other writers act as gatekeepers or else are working to be influential with editors. Why not, then, plan to win some of these people as friends in the manner just described for socially skilled cultivation of criticism? Gatekeepers are easily contacted. Their names appear on journal mastheads, on book reviews; they tend to be salient people. Send them formative examples of your work and ask for their specific advice and direction. Persist; many of them have managed success by ignoring all but the most sincere and appropriate requests for help. They, by virtue of their success, probably found a few writers who helped them at critical points in their careers.

Equally important, cultivate exchanges of formative materials with aspiring authors. Learn from them. Use them (and let them use you) as sources of appreciation.

Develop a sense of audience–As you solicit more criticism, especially from writers you admire and who work on similar topics, you'll learn to anticipate their reactions to your writing. When you can prepare and write your manuscripts with those specific readers in mind, your skill in developing a sense of audience will profit. I encourage writers to pause and carry on imaginary dialogs with these predictable critics–and with less predictable groups of strangers about plans to write. Will they be interested? Will they see your main points readily? How would they want you to change your finished manuscript? And so on.

Writing with a sense of audience does not necessarily mean pandering to readers. It means communicating your ideas, whether readers like them or not, in clear fashion and with clear benefit of your supporting arguments. It means noticing where you're not being understood. It means anticipating differing levels of involvement and background by readers. And it means learning that unintentional miscommunications can unnecessarily offend some readers.

Sense of audience, finally, needs to be treated with the same wariness appropriate to any self-generated concept. It needs regular scrutiny, from the part of you that stands back as a detached, objective observer, to see if it shows signs of health: Does your sensed audience generate positive affect? (If it makes you feel angry or apprehensive, you may need more work on cognitive self-control and on building a helpful social network.) Is it narrowly dependent on one or a few imaginary readers? Or can it scan, when appropriate, to a realistic variety of potential critics? Do you, in fact, listen? Or do you treat imaginary audiences as some writers treat outlines–as something conveniently ignored once writing is under way?

The Four-Step Plan Applied Across Stages of Writing

The third and fourth steps of the Four-Step Plan differ from the first two steps in a critical way: Automaticity and externality seem to work best with the results-first approach, whereas self-control and sociality do not. The last two steps require, as we have just seen, considerable planning and practice before they function effectively.

This difference may explain the relative rarity of cognitive self-control and of social skills approaches to blocking. Automaticity and externality are largely unthinking and effortless; once in place, they produce easy and visible improvements in writing. Changes in our negative scripts of thinking or in our social patterns of writing, in contrast, do not occur so instantaneously.

But improvements in cognitive self-control and in sociality do occur more easily, in my experience, than most writers suppose. My ongoing research suggests that the initially stubborn patterns of negative thinking and of unsocialized writing can be restructured with 10-12 weeks of regular work.

The most telling result of that research confirms a point just made: real progress relies most heavily on planfulness and practice.

Ways to put planfulness and practice into effect are demonstrated in the examples that follow. I recommend following a similar pattern, of trying out the Four-Step Plan until the new patterns of self-control and sociality work comfortably and reliably. Ultimately, with continued replanning and practice, the new patterns become habitual.

Starting a New Project

The emphases in starting a new project remain the same as when we focused on automaticity and externality; i.e., learning to write before feeling ready and learning ways to ensure regular productivity. The addition of the third and fourth steps may not seem so critical here as in later stages of writing. However, self-control and sociality work best as integral parts of writing from the outset. Without them, new starts may induce overt blocking or else implant the discomfort and loneliness that delay and discomfort the writer.

Step 1: Automaticity–Begin with the usual approach: Results-first tactics. Jump right into the project with spontaneous and generative writing techniques. Continue in step- wise fashion until the emerging ideas grow into conceptual outlines and into rough drafts.

If you really aren't ready to begin, consider developing a related form of automaticity called *automatic note taking*. Organize each literature source or other idea source onto separate sheets of paper. Limit your notes, with rare exceptions, to a single page for each source. Compose the page as though talking aloud, as though describing exactly what aspects of the source you can use in your planned project.

With practice, automatic note taking evolves into a rapid, painless procedure for preparing materials. It excludes unnecessary note taking. It discourages unnecessary reading; scanning for relevant materials is usually sufficient. And it allows some mental laziness; once you've spotted the critical materials in a source, you can simply copy them word for word.

Automatic note taking (ANT) produces advantages that relate to stimulus control notions as well. Its single page format and its focus on usable material amount to "limit-setting;" with ANT in effect, you'll be less likely to delay projects with perfectionistic reading of entire sources, you'll have relevant materials organized in succinct form, and you'll save time. Equally important, ANT builds momentum and discipline. I recommend it for writers who are in the depths of reblocking, especially those who suppose themselves incapable of generating ideas.

The annotated bibliography on blocking that appears at the end of this book is an example of automatic note taking; i.e., notes made somewhat unthinkingly, quickly . . . but usefully.

Step 2: Externality–Use the priority principle to make writing or prewriting activities more likely.

Step 3: Self-control–Keep thought-list sheets of the self-talk that occurs immediately prior to scheduled writing sessions. Categorize the self-talk on a continuum of adaptiveness–neutrality–maladaptiveness. Put special emphasis on identifying habitual scripts in negative self-talk and on analyzing the effects of those scripts. Done properly, this takes only a minute or two.

Step 4: Sociality–Arrange social contracts for getting a writing project started. At the least, schedule mutually quiet times when you and another writer meet to work independently. Better yet, schedule regular meetings in which you'll generate a collaborative writing project. The collaborative plan works best, in my experience, when neither participant feels compelled to be fully prepared or ready in the early meetings.

If you are beginning alone, plan to share your ideas with other writers no later than the conceptual outline phase of generative writing. Better yet, share formative plans, in brief format, with editors; better to know early on if you're on track.

Step 5: Collecting data–The fifth step of a four-step plan must, of course, be presented unofficially. I suggest that you collect data–the charts of productivity already described, the self-assessments of problem tendencies, systematic self-ratings of changes in self-talk and in social patterns. If you will act as both a practitioner (i.e., your own blocking therapist) and as a scientist (i.e., a data collector who insists on measurable improvement or else revised plans), you'll help ensure greater benefits.[11] Equally important, your records can act as rewarding reminders of your discipline and progress.

Knowing how aversive data collection is for some writers, however, convinces me that the fifth step should be taken as nothing more than a well-intentioned suggestion.

Resuming a Disrupted Project

Most of us have, stuck away in our files, disrupted writing projects that we should resume. But disrupted projects present a vivid example of how difficult inertia is to overcome; usually, the longer the disruption, the stronger the inhibitions about resumption. As a rule, the Four-Step Plan works best in linear fashion with resumed projects. Where powerful issues make resumption too difficult, though, begin with Step 3 (i.e., cognitive restructuring).

Step 1: Automaticity–I recommend using the already finished portions of the manuscript as a basis for *automatic rewriting*. That is, use those pages as a guide for relatively unthinking regeneration of similar but new pages. Two benefits emerge almost immediately: a) a sense of momentum and b) a sense of familiarity with the old material (i.e., what you were saying and, often, what you were thinking when you wrote it in earlier efforts).

Other benefits follow from a patient extension of automatic rewriting into other forms of automaticity. Refamiliarization may produce concerns about overlooked sources; some respecification of related sources in an automatic note taking format usually helps. Refamiliarization might also produce concerns about conceptual organization; regressive steps, like translating the manuscript back into conceptual outlines, will try your patience, but they can help transform disrupted manuscripts into more viable projects. As a rule, the very fear that may help us avoid a disrupted project, discovering that it was misdirected, can in fact be shown to be exaggerated. And, if your worst suspicions are confirmed (and then reconfirmed by other readers), you can discard the old project with a clear conscience.

Step 2: Externality–Employ as much stimulus control as you need to stick with the project. Above all, emphasize limit-setting. Emphasize its conventional aspects where you schedule strict limits on how much time you'll devote to each stage of resumption; blockers are, in my experience, especially likely to "dawdle" over revisions of specific parts of resumed manuscripts. Then, emphasize the unconventional aspect of limit-setting: Disarm impatience by scheduling a moderate investment in every stage of resumption including automatic rewriting and conceptual outlining.

Step 3: Self-control–Log the self-talk that discourages resumption including, in so far as practical, the inner discourse that occurred when you quit the project in prior efforts. Look for patterns that may relate to usual writing problems, especially procrastination, impatience, and perfectionism. Try to identify the inner discourse that helps produce negative affect.

But most important, search for possible differences between the time when you were disrupted and the time when you resumed the project. Proceed optimistically and look for positive changes. You are, after all, beginning to operate in a different fashion. Are you now more confident, less stymied by concerns over public evaluation of your writing? Were you, in retrospect, more bothered before by dysphoria? Can you, as you observe the negative self-talk that accompanies your efforts to resume an old paper, begin to defuse its irrationality and unhelpfulness?

Writing down self-talk helps objectify and control it.

Step 4: Sociality–The worrisome sense of responsibility for some disrupted projects, especially scholarly or informational projects, can be diffused by enlisting another author as a collaborator. Your offer of collaboration may be more attractive than you suppose: The project is already under way. The prospect of completing and publishing it may be even more important to the collaborator than to you. A social commitment to meet regularly will ensure the momentum that might otherwise come with difficulty.

If you choose to work alone, begin with some feedback from other writers on what you've already written, on your imperfect revisions, or on your newly produced conceptual outlines. Tell your readers that the material is not only unfinished but disrupted. Let them know that you're concerned about having been on the right track before and, possibly, that you're not sure why you lost interest. Don't apologize; other writers will understand and sympathize with your dilemma.

Use that feedback to make judgments on the need to redirect or even discard the project. But be careful to solicit constructive, supportive advice, in part by picking at least some humane readers and, better yet, by asking critics for specific and useful information on what they liked. Be sure to add thanks while you're at it; reviewing is typically a thankless task. How do you identify a poor reviewer? Look for someone whose comments are extreme when other reviewers take a more moderate stance. Look for someone whose primary criticism is that you didn't produce the project that he or she would have. Look for someone who won't make criticisms specific.

[Step 5: Data collecting]

Rejected Projects

When I recheck the records of my conversations with the recalled graduates I mentioned at the beginning of this chapter, the problem of editorial rejections ranks a close second to general aversiveness of writing. No doubt of it, rejections help maintain the aversiveness of writing. This transcript from one of those meetings typifies the point:

- "Things really didn't seem too bad until I got a paper rejected so. . . .well, so rejectingly. [laughs] Even though I knew it would probably happen sooner or later, I wasn't prepared for how much it would hurt. You see [while showing the editor's rejection letter] that it could be worse in a way. I've had reviewers say far more insulting things. What really makes me mad is that the one reviewer didn't understand my paper. He rejected it for the wrong reason." [in response to my question about how the rejection makes him feel]

- "Pretty angry. Discouraged. Not sure what to do next. I mean, how do you proceed when you have to deal with reviewers who don't even take the time to read your stuff carefully, who are so quick to assume that you're incompetent? I mean, it makes me feel like quitting."

Most of us, I suspect, recognize the scenario. While it may be best in the short run to move to an alternative writing project, I recommend working in direct and nearly immediate fashion with editorial rejections. It's a good time, as they say in the horse business, to get right back in the saddle.

Notice that in this case the usual linearity of the Four-Step Plan is readjusted, both in terms of order and in terms of boundaries of the steps. In actual practice, the Four-Step Plan demands the same flexibility as does writing.

Step 1: Externality–Preplanning is perhaps most critical; assume that most of your writing projects will be rejected, at least initially. That plan puts you in touch with reality. It also helps you prepare alternatives. (You can and should rehearse your self-talk; we'll discuss that shortly.) You can plan ways to deal with the rejected manuscript; make prior decisions about where you'll send the manuscript next. Decide that, no matter how seemingly inappropriate the rejection, you'll thank the editor and that wherever possible, you'll try to learn something from the rejecting comments.

Put firm limits on your schedule for revision and resubmission once you have the rejection. Once again, employ sufficient degrees of stimulus control to stay on schedule.

Then, plan for one more contingency: If the rejection does seem fair, suspend the plans just outlined until you've taken a social step.

Share the rejected manuscript and the editorial comments with other writers. Ask their advice (while remembering that it, like the editorial comments, will be nothing more than opinion, not fact) about the wisdom of revising and resubmitting. You may be pleasantly surprised. In nearly 85% of the cases in which writers with whom I worked carried out this directive, they received encouragement and helpful advice on possible revisions and on alternative outlets for the manuscript.

Step 2: Self-control–Here again, anticipate the rejection. Write out your own evaluation of the manuscript, as though you were editor of the journal or publishing house. Sometimes, such a self-evaluation produces practical, cost-effective changes before submission. (Watch out for perfectionism!) Sometimes this self-appraisal acts as a reminder that perfection is not the goal; your manuscript may make worthwhile contributions despite its imperfection. In any case, self-criticism helps provoke the self-talk that will be elicited by editorial rejection.

Write down your anticipated self-talk about the rejection, especially the negative scripts. Get on with the usual procedures of cognitive therapy: Check for negative affect, for irrational thoughts, for patterns of thinking that lead to blocking. Calm down, slow down, as you challenge the irrational thoughts with questions about their logic and helpfulness. Replace the negative thoughts with more positive, helpful thoughts that will encourage and reward writing–both in your self-talk and on the pages where you recorded the negative self-talk. Then, do it over again. Thought substitution requires repeated practice.

Last, but not least, put these rehearsals into effect if and when the rejection arrives. Enforce this with externality; don't, for example, even open the editorial letter until you've already started a thought-list sheet. Without that sort of planfulness, all your efforts and good intentions may evaporate.

Step 3: Automaticity–Begin revising as though resuming a disrupted project. Use automatic rewriting to generate freshness, even a new "voice" in the manuscript if it seems appropriate. Use generative writing, especially conceptual outlining, to develop a sense of whether your original direction and goals were actually clear; you may discover that the reviewers, even the rudest and least understanding, had a point.

As you move back to automaticity, ask a question like this: "Is it possible that I'm responsible, in part at least, for the confusion and/or anger expressed by the reviewers?" If you do, however, be sure to add a positive suggestion like this: "I want to be sure to stay in touch with what it was about the paper that excited me originally, what I knew was worth communicating, and what I suspected would elicit subjective responses in reviewers."

Step 4: Sociality–Ask for opinions from other writers. Listen to their encouragement and to their recollections of similar rejections. Misery loves company. More important, sometimes: Ask the editor and his or her reviewers for *more* criticism. Begin your request with a compliment; i.e., find something about the rejection that helped (or could help) you and thank them for their efforts. Then, ask for more helpful criticism, especially where the original comments were vague (e.g., "sophomoric," "sloppy"). Ask in calm, objective fashion as though your only goal were to gain more useful information.

Don't apologize for your failings. And, don't put your reviewers/ editor on the defensive.

As a rule, this form of socially skilled writing brings at least three benefits, including a) a calmer, though still rejected, writer; b) more useful information on ways to revise your manuscript; and c) reviewers/editors who may treat you more graciously in the future.

I assure you that editors generally dislike sending rejections. But they will remember and perhaps even admire the rare writer who responds with gratitude and with reasonable requests for help.

[Step 5: Collecting data]

Working on Lengthy Projects

Many of the things that make writing difficult, such as the lack of short-term rewards, work even more powerfully as writers undertake longer projects. Some writers I've known blocked only on book-length projects; with shorter projects they worked efficiently. My recent work with writers who have moved to longer projects suggests that the Four-Step Plan can be especially helpful.

Step 1: Automaticity–At first glance, automaticity seems to offer little here, especially to the writer whose project is well under way and thoroughly preplanned. But, in fact, automaticity can help in a most critical way, with maintaining momentum. I suggest developing a series of unthinking rituals to begin each writing session: First, do something that simultaneously relaxes and energizes you while encouraging "right-brained dominance." Pick something unconnected with writing;

e.g., many successful writers take a ritualistic walk before writing, a stroll through pleasant surroundings. Burned-out writers, in contrast, tend to make writing a tense activity.

Second, when you've finished walking or stretching or meditating or whatever, add a brief ritual connected to writing. Avoid lengthy cleaning rituals; instead, make a habit of sharpening your pencils, of arranging your materials, etc.

Third, begin writing by rewriting the last page from the previous session. Resist the temptation of supposing that the last page needs no rewriting. Even if it doesn't, rewriting establishes momentum and re-establishes the mental set of the last session. By the time you begin a new page, you'll probably be writing effortlessly; it's much easier to write when your self-talk is generating content for writing than when generating self-conscious doubts about writing.

Step 2: Externality–Establish enough stimulus control so that you write regularly, preferably four or five days a week on your long project. Use time-management techniques to arrange regular times even if some days permit no more than 15- to 20-minute sessions. Establish limited writing times on other days where you might otherwise binge.

Emphasize the planning of meaningful, measurable sub-goals (e.g., completion of one chapter) that can be met at intervals no longer than four or five planned sessions. Then, be clear (e.g., use charts) about when you've met your sub-goals and institute some kind of reward. Use the same sort of planning for sub-goals to set limits against dawdling.

Arrange brief, unobtrusive writing tasks that can be completed while your long project drags on. It helps to see that you can still finish things. If you can't think of a brief project, you may be too invested in the long one.

Look about for brief, alternative tasks like book reviews. Yes, it's true that most book reviews are by invitation only; it's also true that some reviewers gain entry by sending editors a non-demanding indication of interest in reviewing.

Step 3: Self-control–Lengthy writing projects encourage almost all bad scripts to get worse. Self-talk about the wisdom of procrastinating grows more convincing. Self-talk reminding you how slowly you're progressing becomes more devastating. Obsessiveness and excessive self-reflection can even make a manuscript seem foreign, like someone else's writing, or else so overly familiar that it becomes embarrassing. Sometimes the writing itself becomes the source of chronic dysphoria.

So it is, in my experience, that writers who can manage brief projects by ignoring their self-talk must often learn to deal with it in completing book-length manuscripts. One script, more than any other, merits attention: Beware of the voice that tells you, in effect, that bigger projects must necessarily bring bigger risks of failure. Preplan for such self-doubts with realistic answers. Build a collection of anecdotes about the greater rewards of publishing longer projects. Schedule simultaneous work on briefer projects. Arrange alternative uses for your long project (e.g., separate publication of parts of the project), regardless of its eventual publishability.

Step 4: Sociality–You can anticipate the basic advice I'll give here; i.e., share unfinished portions of your project with supportive readers.

Long projects also necessitate frequent checking of sense of audience: "Have I strayed off course? Do I continue to write for myself *and* for a realistic audience?"

Another bit of advice may be unexpected. Plan to resist social pressures to write more quickly and magically. Non-writers (and even some unblocked writers) suppose that good writing occurs almost instantaneously. They also assume that writers who take longer are both lazy and socially irresponsible. They harass writers with ostensibly innocent comments like this: "Are you *still* working on that book?" (They seem to assume that a 500-page manuscript can be produced in a week or two.)

Deal with this social pressure in two ways: First, recognize that the "*still*" is an implied criticism. Respond, as with all criticisms, by agreeing, calmly and reflectively. Agree that it seems to take forever. Ask for even more criticism, vaguely, with something like "Isn't that awful?" With that simple strategy, you can defuse the criticism and help remove the pressures to write more quickly.

Second, take your own writing time more seriously. Regard it as something that you *have* to do, as something that no reasonable person will question. I encourage writers to visualize the behavior of someone who really does consider his or her work important. A physician, for example, who leaves a social gathering for regular hospital rounds receives little social pressure, in part because if hassled, he or she would respond with righteous indignation. Why shouldn't writers command much of the same consideration?

[Step 5: Collecting data]

Difficulties and Individualizations

The Four-Step Plan differs from usual remedies for blocking in its scope; i.e., it offers an integrated, demanding set of solutions. Its limitation, in my experience, rests mostly with its demandingness. The Four-Step Plan asks writers to carry out an increasingly complex and self-directed regimen, the more so with Steps 3 and 4. Self-control and sense of sociality must ultimately be self-regenerated.

But, ongoing research shows that it works. The Four-Step Plan helps writers do the very things that the names of the steps suggest. And not only do records of self-talk, for example, indicate real and lasting displacement of negative scripts, but the notes of these writers show how they generalize specific procedures across writing situations. They find new uses for automaticity, such as the prewriting rituals just mentioned. They come to sessions with exciting accounts of such innovations, with suggestions for other writers. Gradually, almost imperceptibly, our roles begin to change. I learn from them. They become their own writing facilitators.

My study with writers who work largely on their own, with materials similar to those in this book, suggests that they respond in nearly identical fashion. The difference, if any, is that the "home-based" writers move more quickly toward acting as their own writing facilitators. They take more initiative in applying their blocking assessments and other experience to individualization of their four-step plan.

Chronic procrastinators, for instance, find ways to apply all four steps to their problematic tendency; they learn that planfulness is the chief enemy of procrastination. Equally important, they get in touch with the factors, internal and external, that encourage procrastination. They forgive themselves for being procrastinators, they defuse criticisms of their "bad" habit, and they work, patiently, on a broad-spectrum plan to make writing more comfortable.

Writers who do this conscientiously, in my experience, learn to apply their writing self-therapy in unanticipated ways. One writer, for instance, was recently able to see that writing, as enjoyable and valuable as it had become for him, needed a temporary reassignment of priority. He realized that the expected arrival of a child demanded much, but not all, of his usual writing times. I agreed. Writing should never, in my opinion, take precedence over things like healthy social needs.

Notes

[1]Boice, R. (1985). Cognitive components of blocking. *Written Communication, 2*, 91-104.

[2]See, for example: Boice, R., Pecker, G., & Shaughnessy, P. (1985). Women and publishing in psychology. *American Psychologist, 40*, 577-578.

[3]Rico, G. L. (1983). *Writing the natural way*. Los Angeles: J. P. Tarcher.

[4]Ornstein, R. E. (1977). *The psychology of consciousness*. New York: Harcourt Brace Jovanovich.

[5]Watson, D. L., & Tharp, R. G. (1972). *Self-directed behavior: Self-modification for personal adjustment*. Monterey, CA. Brooks/Cole.

[6]Liddy, G. G. (1981). *Will*. New York: Dell.

[7]Meichenbaum, D., & Cameron, R. (1974). The clinical potential of modifying what clients say to themselves. In M. J. Mahoney & C. E. Thoreson (Eds.), *Self-control*. Monterey, CA: Brooks/Cole.

[8]See, for example: Beck, A. T., Rush, A. J., Shaw, B. F., & Emery, G. (1979). *Cognitive therapy of depression*. New York: Guilford Press.

[9]Boice, R., Barlow, D. H., Johnson, K., & Klosko, J. (1984). Behaviorists as peer reviewers: Do they misbehave? *The Behavior Therapist, 7*, 105-107.

[10]Curran, J. P., & Monti, P. M. (1982). *Social skills training*. New York: Guilford Press.

[11]Barlow, D. H., Hayes, S. C., & Nelson, R. O. (1984). *The scientist practitioner*. New York: Pergamon Press.

SECTION D:
Beyond Solutions,
to Growth

Introduction

A SURPRISINGLY HARD PART of carrying out a program with professors as writers is termination. Once writers have mastered the Four-Step Plan, they usually don't need more regular sessions with me. It's too bad, in a way; by that point, we carry on delightful conversations. We are more likely to discuss ideas for writing than obstacles to writing. I do very little work.

But when we set end points, a note of unpleasantness often creeps in. Some writers feel abandoned. They wonder how they'll function without my regular support and prodding. They worry about relapses; surely, they suppose, writing won't always come so easily.

Chapter 8 compiles the information and advice I've found effective during the later stages of my writing programs. Stated simply, this last chapter helps prepare writers for independence by emphasizing independent means of growth. It focuses on the most pervasive concern of writers at this point—fears of relapsing into writing problems.

Chapter Eight

Dealing with Relapses

MY EARLIEST ACQUAINTANCE with relapses was with "backsliding." It was what people did when they strayed from the strict rules of religion. While backsliding wasn't condoned, it was understood; an evil world teeming with temptations made backsliding seem forgivable. The backslider who returned with a public confession brought joy to the congregation.

There is, I suspect, a lesson in that recollection. Deep down, we expect people to fail, especially at something as difficult and righteous as writing. We may even welcome occasional failures as evidence that frailties plague us all. So it is, I assume, that our culture abounds with stories of successful writers who suddenly and mysteriously stopped writing. It seems almost natural.

I object to the traditional notion that writing problems are inevitable, that sooner or later writers will dry up or burn out. When writing habits incorporate extrinsic and intrinsic satisfactions, when they produce continuing growth in skillfulness and success, why would writers lapse? I can imagine no good reason (unless, of course, there really is a Muse who whimsically gives and takes away a writer's ideas and motivations).

So far as I can see, successful writers who remain physically and emotionally healthy rarely relapse. Consider some of the examples: Will and Ariel Durant, Agatha Christie, Isaac Asimov. Conversely, authors who write with unhappy motives and with unhealthy habits such as alcoholism often fall prey to blocking. F. Scott Fitzgerald and Ernest Hemingway come to mind.

Indeed, relapses occur much like any other aspect of writing problems–in understandable and manageable ways. Relapses can be avoided, in my experience, by extending the tactics we have already discussed to a more studied perspective.

What Causes/Predisposes Relapses

Relapsing carries another traditional connotation besides inevitability; it generally is used to mean that the miscreant "knew better." An obvious place to begin our coverage of causes, then, is with an account of what, in common parlance, might be called dropping your guard.

Lack of Planfulness

Ongoing surveys of "graduates" from my writing programs indicate a single, most common correlate of relapsing into blocking–abandonment of planfulness, especially in terms of continuing to arrange external controls and schedules for writing.

If planfulness in arranging externality works so well, why do writers abandon it? Almost all these respondents recalled something that preceded the decision to drop externality–a conviction that intrinsic motivation and internal controls should be sufficient. They had wearied of forcing themselves to write, of feeling weak about having to manufacture their resolve.

But further questioning revealed another reason for dropping externality, one that offers more hope of helping writers prevent relapses. Almost all of the relapsed writers recalled something else that happened before they talked themselves out of relying on externality; they had grown disillusioned with writing.

Disillusionment

Writers, in my experience, tend to be idealists. They enjoy living at least parts of their lives in worlds of ideas and ideals. They embrace romantic notions including the expectation of a Muse who makes writing magically clever and easy, magically appreciated and rewarded. Things usually don't work out this way, of course, and once that realization settles in, so can bitterness.

The most tempting target for that bitterness, so far as I can tell, is with the system of externally imposed discipline. When I listen to relapsed writers describe their feelings about the program that has seemingly failed them, I am reminded of other groups of people I've known who've wanted to change. Formerly obese people, when struck with some of the same old social failures, often resort to old patterns of binge-eating. They vent their anger on the program. I don't take the criticisms personally; I sympathize with their disappointments, and I know that some of their anger is temporary.

Traumas

Traumas finished a surprising third in surveyed reasons for relapsing. In fact, very few former participants re-experienced writing problems due to unanticipated disappointments and stressors. While they might have put writing aside until things were taken care of or until an illness had passed, most of these writers resumed writing at the first practical opportunity.

This pattern held in surprising cases, even where the death of someone close to a writer might have disrupted and even blocked writing; instead, these writers reported a stronger desire for activities like writing that distracted them from their losses.

All but one of the few cases of traumas associated with writing problems might better be categorized with disillusionment or with lack of planfulness. Three writers remained stuck for at least a month upon receiving strong editorial rejections. None of these relapsed writers had employed cognitive rehearsals to anticipate the rejections and none tried to use externality in any serious way to resume writing. Instead, they focused on the negativity and rejectingness of the editorial remarks. When they showed me the offending reviews, I agreed. They had been ill- treated. But I also, as you would anticipate, offered some suggestions about other ways of coping with rejection.

Some Ways to Combat Relapses into Blocking

One pattern characterizes all the former participants who relapsed into real problem patterns. They carried implicit expectations that, sooner or later, they would fail. And, they knew better. That is, they all possessed the techniques and the experience to prevent reblocking. They knew how to maintain planfulness. They knew how to deal with disillusioning thoughts.

What made them different from the writers I surveyed who showed few propensities to re-experience writing problems? The main factor could be labeled a readiness to generalize experience and insight to new situations.[1] Writers who have not relapsed appear to be more willing to take the risk of trying techniques like the Four-Step Plan in non-anticipated ways. Relapsers, in contrast, are clearly no less intelligent or knowledgeable, but they are more hesitant to make techniques like cognitive self-control a general part of their lives.

Why do relapsers resist the sort of generalization that could help prevent reblocking? My interviews with them suggest several interrelated possibilities: These writers want to keep writing separate from their other concerns. They would like to be able to handle new writing problems without the crutch of programs and techniques. And they lose patience with writing that demands so much flexibility and hard work but, initially at least, gives so little in return.

Systematic follow-up work with these relapsed writers, however, indicates that they are easily won back to the congregation of satisfied and productive writers. The strategies that seem most effective in preventing further relapses follow. I present them in the format I now use with writers just ending writing programs–before relapses typically occur.

Combine Externality and Internality

The Four-Step Plan works even more effectively, in my experience, when writers aim to combine the techniques of external control and self-control. That is, if they continue to maintain sufficient levels of externality such as scheduling writing times and sub-goals even after they feel they have mastered cognitive self-control, they are less likely to relapse. And, it follows, they fare better if they abandon the common dream of having all the control and reward for writing be intrinsic.

Why is this so important? Evidently, few if any of us ever really master self-control so thoroughly in regard to writing that we can work effectively without externality. We need to continue practicing externality, not just as a back-up, but as a means of maintaining sound and unthinking habits. Even long-established writers such as Irving Wallace create "artificial discipline" for themselves.[2] It makes life easier.

But mastery may require a special kind of self-discipline; i.e., admission that we are not perfect, that we can't do it all by ourselves.

This kind of admission helps, evidently, in applying combined techniques of externality and internality in the generalized fashion just described.

I don't have firm evidence as yet, but I expect to demonstrate that externality and internality must act in concert for the best effects on writing. In other words, if you want the advantages of self-control, you should begin with and stay with externally arranged controls.

Work at Keeping Writing in Perspective

When I've gotten past the advice about combining and generalizing techniques for unblocking, I usually say something that surprises me: Resist the temptation to give writing too high a priority. It shouldn't take precedence over one's health and social needs.

Watch for signs of burnout in writing: a) dysphoria, b) tedium, and c) cynicism. Better yet, head off burnout with planfulness. Don't overdo writing just because you're feeling impatient or insecure. Stick to a reasonable schedule. Write about some things you enjoy. And work at abandoning foolish ideals about writing; foolish idealism, is after all, a major predictor of burnout.[3]

Face Up to the Hard Realities of Writing

Face it: Life isn't always fair. Especially for writers.

Then, recognize that you can deal with the hard realities of writing while maintaining an appreciation of writing's rewards. With the sort of balance outlined in the following examples, writers become more resistant to disillusionment.[4]

Writing is hard work–Yes, I realize that you already know that. But, do you apply that knowledge when it helps (e.g., when feeling impatient)? Writing also brings enormous rewards such as public recognition. Why should it be different from any other complex and worthwhile challenge?

Writing brings frequent disappointment–Not all ideas for writing come to fruition. Much writing is rejected for publication. Most published writing is either unappreciated or misunderstood. But writing allows a unique kind of self- education, regardless of its publishability. And, in fact, writers who persist rarely fail to find some audience.

Writing elicits hostility–It's probably true that the gatekeepers of publication reject too harshly and too arbitrarily. But abandoning attempts to write merely helps perpetuate that system. Consider spending some of your energies as I do, in researching and writing about editorial systems.[5] But, whatever, don't let insensitive and prejudiced people keep you from writing. Instead, try to learn from them.

When I'm discussing this point with writers, I find one anecdote especially effective. I recently conducted a survey of some of the most visible authors and most powerful editors in the social sciences about their views on writing and publishing. They responded in near unison to one question about what keeps the vast majority of social scientists from writing for publication. They said, in effect, that . . .

> "The reason that most people don't write for publication is because they have nothing to say."

In other words, they seem to be elitists who suppose that almost no one else is worth listening to.

Only a few of them listed other possibilities such as discrimination, lack of opportunity, and discouraging reviewers. Instead, they concluded that the people who really need to write already do. Not surprisingly, many of these same respondents held similar attitudes about the value of programs to help unblock writers. One editor said it most directly:

> "Why bother? Too much is already being written and good writers don't need help."

When you think about it, these elitist views are understandable. Why shouldn't the minority of people who do the majority of writing feel that they alone have the special "calling" to write? Why shouldn't they, armed with increasingly easier successes, forget how difficult writing once was? Why shouldn't they resist a democratization of the writing process?

While we might understand the elitism of already successful writers, we don't need to accept their hostility. Instead, I urge writers to react indignantly to this survey outcome. They typically report using the thought as a motivation to remain unblocked and to break into print.

Work on Writing Skills

One good defense against the elitists is a good offense. Learn to play the writing game, at least part of it, according to their rules. Many of their rules appear in print, especially suggestions for writing well.[6]

Guides to good writing (such as Strunk and White's *Elements of Style*)[7] abound. So do reluctances to use them. Most problem writers I've known despise style guides. Images of priggish writing teachers come to mind.

The style guides appear to be written so perfectly, so tightly that they remind writers of their own unskillfulness. Most important, style guides overwhelm readers with a mass of seemingly trivial rules. "Do I really," one writer remarked after looking over Strunk and White, "want to get invested in details like remembering that 'enthuse' is an 'annoying verb growing out of the noun enthusiasm'?" I agreed that it seemed a bit trivial.

Style guides can help if you put them into realistic perspective. Recognize, as Peter Elbow[8] does, that the people who take rules about grammar and style most seriously, composition teachers, are good candidates for writing problems, especially perfectionism.

Then, work in compromise fashion. Concentrate on a few practical suggestions for stylistic improvement.

The brief list that follows comes from my research on the editorial process; I've chosen the things that, in unskilled form, tend to dispose reviewers to see manuscripts as unsophisticated.

Wordiness–Cut unnecessary words. Learn to recognize wordiness by looking for redundant words and passages. Find ways to combine ideas into single, brief sentences. Use more pronouns. And practice cutting excess verbiage on other people's papers; wordiness shows up more obviously when you read someone else's writing.

Active verbs–Avoid overuse of the verb to be. Use more active verbs.

Locate subjects and verbs near the beginning of most sentences, preferably close together.

Focus–Examine sentences, then paragraphs, then sections, etc., to check for shifts in your subject. In the short run, you can ensure fewer shifts in the subject by writing in the first person; then, there can be no doubt about the subject's identity. In the longer run, use conceptual outlines to ensure the logical flow of your topic through paragraphs and sections.

Shorter paragraphs and clear "signposts" such as more sub-headings–These appeal to the reader's eye and they give the appearance of clearer focus and direction. Remember that readers, even reviewers, tend to be lazy. They scan. They form quick impressions. And when reading doesn't proceed easily, with a clear sense of focus and direction, readers blame the writer.

Avoid unsophisticated usages–Reviewers in academe especially dislike the misuse of words like data, phenomena, and criteria as singular (cf. datum, phenomenon, criterion). Yes, they're being picayune. But why offend them over something so unimportant?

Revise–Read your finished manuscript into a tape recorder. Then, listen for awkward transitions, dysfluencies, etc., and mark the manuscript for later consideration.

Strive for parallel and balanced rhythms[9]–As you learn to be better listener to your own writing, your cadences and resonances will become more obvious and more important.

Model–Cherish good writing like Russell Baker's,[10] Truman Capote's,[11] Joan Didion's,[12] etc. Actively emulate the parts of their styles that appeal to you. Experiment.

But don't overdo it. You won't need to write as well as they do to achieve success in writing. Most important . . .

Write about things that enthuse you.
And, don't take stylistic rules too seriously.

The Best Way to Avoid Relapsing: Missionary Work

My most successful "graduates" have discovered that the best way to learn and ingrain principles for unblocking is to teach those principles to others. I think of it as missionary work. Whatever label you choose, you'll find that this strategy brings enormous benefits and satisfaction. Teaching others means, among other things, that you will:

- understand the concepts, by virtue of having to explain and demonstrate them
- be the subject of appreciation; newly productive and successful writers tend to be very grateful
- be more likely to persist in your writing; your disciples will expect you to practice what you teach.

When I've made this last suggestion to the writers who have worked mostly on their own, with materials like those in this book, an interesting interchange sometimes occurs:

[me] "What do you think? Would it be a good idea to recruit another writer or two, where you help direct them through a program like the one you're completing?"

[writer] "Yeah, probably. But why don't I just give them a copy of the manual? That's how I did it. I did most of it on my own."

[me] "Ah ha! [laughs] You sound like one of the elite writers who suppose that blocked writers should sink or swim on their own. That's not really you, is it?"

[writer] "No. I see what you mean. I might not have made it without at least some extra help. And I know what you're saying is probably true. I'll probably help myself even more than I'll help the blocked writers."

[me] "Good! [laughs] I can rest easy, knowing that I haven't turned out the most dreaded, loathsome writer known to me, an elitist. Seriously, the more experience I have with writing programs, the more convinced I grow that not all writers with something worth saying 'make it' without help. And I expect that some of them, because they've had to struggle to stay productive, will work better with professors as writers than I do."

Notes

[1]See, for example of a similar concept: Crego, C. A., & Crego, M. W. (1983). A training/consultation model of crisis intervention with law enforcement officers. In *Crisis Intervention*. New York: Human Sciences Press.

[2]Wallace, I. (1971). *The writing of one novel*. New York: Simon & Schuster.

[3]Pines, A. M., & Aronson, E. (1981). *Burnout: From tedium to personal growth*. New York: Free Press.

[4]Boice, R., & Jones, F. (1984). Why academicians don't write. *Journal of Higher Education, 55*, 567-582.

[5]Boice, R., Barlow, D. H., Johnson, K., & Klosko, J. (1984). Behaviorists as peer reviewers: Do they misbehave? *The Behavior Therapist, 7*, 105-107.

[6]Selvin, H. C., & Wilson, E. K. (1983). *On sharpening sociologists' prose*. Unpublished manuscript, State University of New York at Stony Brook.

[7]Strunk, W., Jr., & White, E. B. (1979). *The elements of style*. New York: Macmillan.

[8]Elbow, P. (1981). *Writing with power*. New York: Oxford University Press.

[9]Rico, G. L. (1983). *Writing the natural way*. Los Angeles, CA: J. P. Tarcher.

[10]Baker, R. (1984). *Growing up*. New York: New American Library.

[11]Capote, T. (1981). *Music for chameleons*. New York: Signet.

[12]Didion, J. (1981). *Slouching towards Bethlehem*. New York: Washington Square Press.

SECTION E:
Appendices

Part One:

The Blocking Questionnaire:
An Instrument for Assessing
Writing Problems

THE PROBLEM about most information on writing blocks, as Daly[1] notes, is its basis in anecdotes. Daly's own work on writing apprehension stands as the prototype for assessing writing problems with empirical grounding.[2] In this section of the appendices I present a related effort at identifying inhibitions to writing.

The Blocking Questionnaire (BQ) was standardized, in its present form, on two groups of academicians, 100 graduate students and 100 faculty members across a variety of disciplines in large universities. Its items, selected via factor analysis and criterion-related judgments (about writers with clearly diagnosed writing problems and their responses to the BQ), sorted themselves into the same seven categories of blocking identified in earlier research.[3]

I continue to use the BQ as a device to help individualize the treatment programs structured for the professional writers (and non-writers) with whom I work. I share the BQ in hopes of learning how well it discriminates and helps other populations of troubled writers. In the form presented here, the BQ works well as a self-administered diagnostic for writers. Material following the questionnaire explains scoring, interpretation, and application of the results.

I strongly encourage you to "take" the BQ and to score your response patterns. I use the diagnostic categories throughout the manual to provide more individualized advice.

Blocking Questionnaire

A. Checklist for Overt Signs of Blocking (COSB)

Robert Boice (copyright 1984, 1987)
State University of New York, Stony Brook

Please pause briefly with each item, imagine how you would probably
act when faced with a tough and important writing assignment, and
then check the portion of the scale that would best describe you:

(work apprehension)

1. Others would hear me com-
    plain: "I don't feel like do-
    ing this" (or words to that ef-
    fect).

    Never | | | | | | | | | | Always
    0 1 2 3 4 5 6 7 8 9 10

2. Others would hear me com-
    plain about how difficult or
    fatiguing the writing will be.

    Never | | | | | | | | | | Always
    0 1 2 3 4 5 6 7 8 9 10

3. Others would hear me com-
    plain about the difficulties in
    generating useful, significant
    ideas for writing.

    Never | | | | | | | | | | Always
    0 1 2 3 4 5 6 7 8 9 10

4. Others would hear me com-
    plain about the realistic pos-
    sibilities of my writing being
    criticized, even rejected.

    Never | | | | | | | | | | Always
    0 1 2 3 4 5 6 7 8 9 10

[Work Apprehension average score _____ [   ]]

(procrastination)

5. I would put off the writing as long as possible (until just before the deadline, if there is one).

6. I would use delaying tactics such as working first on more "pressing" tasks, like house-cleaning or reading the news-paper.

7. I would, once ready to write, spend a lot of time daydream-ing.

8. Others would hear me com-plain about the agency or people who made the writing task (and deadline) necessary.

[Procastination average score _____ [   ]]

(writing apprehension)

9. Others would hear me ex-press nervousness about writ-ing.

10. Others would notice that when I try to write, I fatigue, even "cramp," easily.

11. Others would hear my wor-ries about not writing as well as my peers.

[Writing Apprehension average score _____ [   ]]

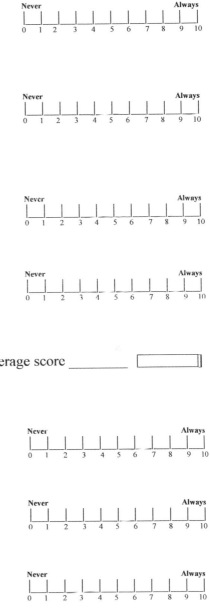

(dysphoria)

12. Others would see that, when faced with writing, I show signs of depression (e.g., sad expression, lethargy, complaints of feeling helpless).

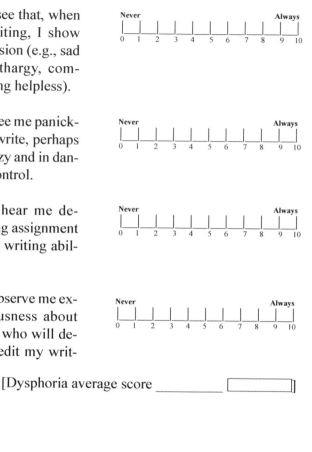

13. Others would see me panicking, unable to write, perhaps even acting dizzy and in danger of losing control.

14. Others would hear me devalue the writing assignment and/or my own writing ability.

15. Others would observe me express suspiciousness about specific people who will deliberately discredit my writing.

[Dysphoria average score _____ ⬚]

(impatience)

16. Others would hear me complain that, once under way, my writing is going too slowly... that I need to make up for lost time.

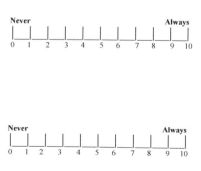

17. Others would hear me express disappointment in not producing good copy easily and quickly.

18. Others would observe that when I do write, I work with few breaks or rest periods, in intense and hurried fashion.

19. Others would observe that I resist taking the extra time to carry out post-writing tasks such as revising, getting informal reviews from friends, proofreading carefully.

[Impatience average score _____ 「_____」]

(perfectionism)

20. Others would observe me doing regular editing (e.g., stopping to correct misspellings) during the first draft.

21. Others would observe me having a hard time finishing a manuscript because I persist in making refinements.

22. Others would hear me worrying that I may have overlooked important literature, or committed some incredible oversight, in writing.

23. Others would see me struggle to include too much information in my manuscript.

[Perfectionist average score _____ 「_____」]

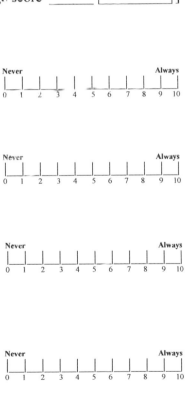

(rules)

24. Others would hear my Negativism about outlining and/or observe that I don't outline before writing (or that if I do, I then ignore the outline).

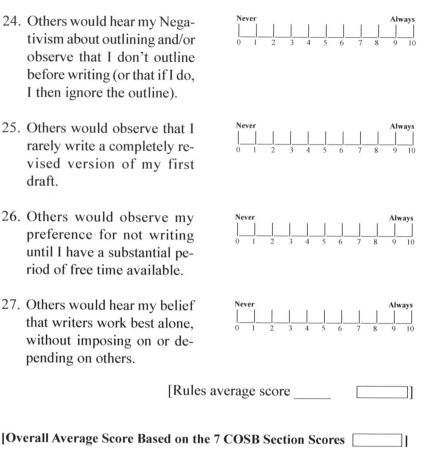

Never   Always
0   1   2   3   4   5   6   7   8   9   10

25. Others would observe that I rarely write a completely revised version of my first draft.

Never   Always
0   1   2   3   4   5   6   7   8   9   10

26. Others would observe my preference for not writing until I have a substantial period of free time available.

Never   Always
0   1   2   3   4   5   6   7   8   9   10

27. Others would hear my belief that writers work best alone, without imposing on or depending on others.

Never   Always
0   1   2   3   4   5   6   7   8   9   10

[Rules average score _____   [   ]]

[**Overall Average Score Based on the 7 COSB Section Scores** [   ]]

B. Checklist of Cognitions/Emotions in Blocking (CCB)

Please pause with each item and imagine that a) you are faced with a tough and important writing task, b) you are getting ready to write, c) you are alone, and d) you are talking to yourself as you prepare to write and that you occasionally stop while writing and engage in further self-talk about the writing task. Please use this scenario to check the most appropriate place on the scale in terms of what you would probably say to yourself. And, finally, please realize that each example of a self-statement is only approximate; it applies to you even if you would state it a bit differently.

(work apprehension) (likelihood I would say something like this to myself)

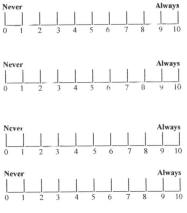

1. "I don't feel like writing." "I don't want to do this."

2. "This is going to be exhausting, tiring." "Writing wears me out."

3. "I have no ideas for writing."

4. "Even if I do a good job, the person (or persons) who evaluates my writing may criticize it for some picky reason."

[Work apprehension average score _____ [   ]]

(procrastination)

5. "I work best when I wait until the last minute." "I've always managed to get papers done under pressure."

6. "I'll wait until I'm feeling more like writing." "I'll feel more like writing if I do something else first."

Never   Always
0 1 2 3 4 5 6 7 8 9 10

7. "If I just relax and think, good ideas for writing may come to me."

Never   Always
0 1 2 3 4 5 6 7 8 9 10

8. "I wish I hadn't agreed to write this paper," and/or "I feel annoyed with 'X' for forcing me to do this."

Never   Always
0 1 2 3 4 5 6 7 8 9 10

[Procrastination average score _____ [   ]]

(writing apprehension)

9. "I feel nervous about starting."

Never   Always
0 1 2 3 4 5 6 7 8 9 10

10. "I'm already exhausted and I'm only beginning," and/or "My wrist is so tight and cramped that it's hard to write."

Never   Always
0 1 2 3 4 5 6 7 8 9 10

11. "I'll bet that 'X' won't like this." "He/she may even laugh at my writing." "I'll feel like a fool."

Never   Always
0 1 2 3 4 5 6 7 8 9 10

12. "I probably won't do as good a job at writing as my peers would." "I just don't match up to what others can do."

Never   Always
0 1 2 3 4 5 6 7 8 9 10

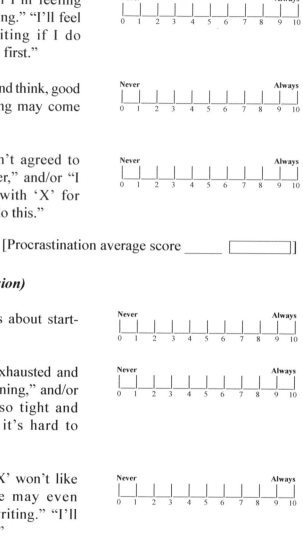

[Writing apprehension average score _____ [   ]]

(dysphoria)

13. "I feel depressed." "This makes me feel so sad I could cry." "This makes me feel really helpless."

14. "I am panicking." "I may be losing control." "I may not be able to catch my breath." "I'm going to be too sick to write."

15. "This is a stupid writing assignment." "Most published writing is pointless." "I have nothing original or worthwhile to say." "I'm never going to be a good writer."

16. "No matter how well I do, there are a few people who will deliberately discredit my writing."

[Dysphoria average score _____ [   ]]

(impatience)

17. "I'm not working fast enough." "I've got too much to do and too little time." "I need to make up for lost time."

18. "If I were working efficiently, writing would come more easily, in more finished form."

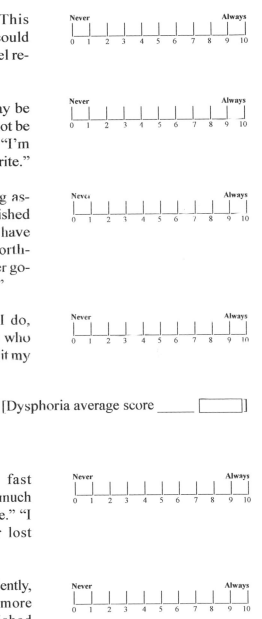

19. "Once I get started, I like to keep working as long as I can." "If I stop for a break, I might lose my train of thought."

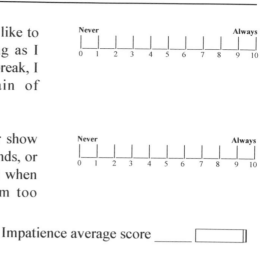

20. "I'd like to revise (or show my manuscript to friends, or proof more carefully) when I'm finished, but I'm too busy."

Impatience average score _____ [   ]

(perfectionism)

21. "I'm not comfortable going on with my first draft unless I stop to correct errors."

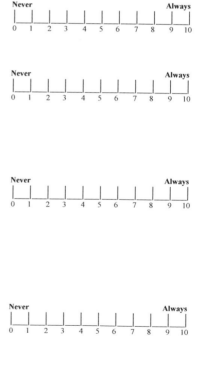

22. "No matter how long I've worked on a paper I like to keep revising and perfecting, even after I suspect the paper is 'good enough.'"

23. "What if I've overlooked something, missed a reference?" "What if someone else has already written a similar paper that I don't know about?"

24. "Once I've gone to the trouble to read an article, I can't stand to leave it out of my review section."

[Perfectionism average score _____ [   ]

(rules)

25. "I hate to outline." "I don't need outlines."

26. "I like to wait until I have an inspiration or a clear idea of what I'm going to say."

27. "I can't write unless I can set aside a large period of time when I have nothing else to do."

28. "I like to write in private, without having to rely on help from others."

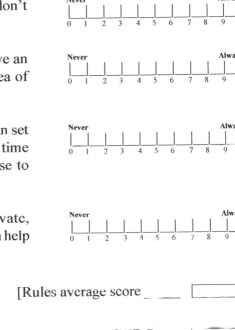

[Rules average score _ _ _

[Overall Average CCB Score

C. Survey of Social Skills in Writing (SSSW)

Please check the extent with which you would engage in the following activities when engaged in a tough and important writing task. (Please note that on this questionnaire, the scoring labels alternate.)

(work apprehension)

1. I would begin by thinking of ways to involve other people as helpers as coauthors, as sources for ideas and inspiration, etc.

2. I would write for myself in-
    stead of a specific, imagined
    audience, at least initially.

[Work apprehenson average score _____ [   ]]

(procrastination)

3. I like to set up a schedule, to
    work around other people
    who are writing.

4. I tend to resent people who
    try to help me with my writ-
    ing, especially if they're
    pushy.

Procastination average score _____ [   ]]

(writing apprehension)

5. I think it's best not to discuss
    my writing problems with
    others.

6. I believe that my writing
    problems are unique to me–
    that few if any other people
    suffer in similar ways.

[Writing apprehension average score _____ [   ]]

(dysphoria)

7. My friends take an active in-
    terest in my writing and feel
    free to offer support and criti-
    cism.

8. I tend to see criticisms of my writing as personal attacks.

Never — 0 1 2 3 4 5 6 7 8 9 10 — Always

[Dysphoria average score _____ [   ]]

(impatience)

9. I try to place as much importance on post-writing tasks (e.g., casual reviews by friends, revising and resubmitting) as on the original writing.

Never — 0 1 2 3 4 5 6 7 8 9 10 — Always

10. I resist the temptation to ask for opinions, etc., before submitting a paper because I'm simply too busy.

Never — 0 1 2 3 4 5 6 7 8 9 10 — Always

[Impatience average score _____ [   ]]

(perfectionism)

11. I find it easy to suppose that others, even friends, will think less of me if they see an example of my poor or erroneous writing.

Never — 0 1 2 3 4 5 6 7 8 9 10 — Always

12. I tend to believe that my writing must be more thoroughgoing and polished than that of my peers.

Never — 0 1 2 3 4 5 6 7 8 9 10 — Always

[Perfectionism average score _____ [   ]]

(rules)

13. I tend to suspect that most people have little to say and, thus, might be better off not writing.

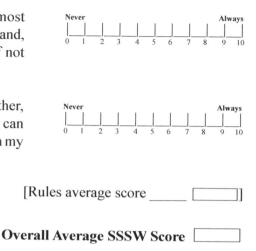

14. I tend to believe that other, less experienced writers, can be helpful collaborators in my own writing projects.

[Rules average score _____ [   ]]

Overall Average SSSW Score [   ]

Scoring

Proceed from the most general to the most specific scoring while considering what the scores mean.

Begin by adding up scores in each of the seven component sections of each of the three questionnaires. Where, for example, a component section on rules (CCB) has four questions, the average score is determined by . . .

a. adding the total (the maximum = 40) and

b. dividing the total by 4 (the maximum = 10)

Then, add the component scores *within* a questionnaire (e.g., CCB) and compute the overall average for that questionnaire (or modality). All questionnaires have seven components, so the average score = the total score divided by seven.

Overall blocking score. Enter the average scores for each questionnaire (i.e., modality) here:

COSB ___ ___ . ___

CCB ___ ___ . ___

SSSW ___ ___ . ___

And then enter the average of the three scores here:

Overall
Blocking Mean   ___ ___ . ___
Score

Interpretation

Overall scores provide a general index of how serious blocking tendencies and problems are relative to other academicians. Preliminary tests with these questionnaires suggest this guide to interpretation:

Score	Interpretation
0 - 2.5	minor problems typical of people already writing productively (i.e., not blocked)
2.6 - 4.5	moderate problems usually more associated with inefficient and somewhat painful writing than with more disruptive blocks
4.6 - 7.0	serious problems; often predictive of disruptive blocks that recur
7.1 - 10.0	blocking often associated with chronic psychological problems such as depression and writing phobias

An unusually high score cautions against quick and easy solutions; it suggests that other, perhaps psychological, problems may need attention. It also warns about probabilities of relapses occurring, even when unblocking seems well under way. If your score is unusually low (and *if* you've been forthright in answering), it can mean that you may be able to move more quickly through initial strategies of unblocking to stages emphasizing painless and successful writing.

But first, you can profit in learning more about specific factors that contribute to your blocking.

Questionnaire scores. Next are modalities of blocking. You've already taken a look at the extent to which you evidence blocking on each of the three questionnaires. Reenter your scores from the preceding section here in terms of . . .

1. your overt behavior (COSB average score) .... ☐☐ . ☐

2. your cognitive and emotional responses
    (CCB average score)...................................... ☐☐ . ☐

3. your social behavior (SSSW average score)......... ☐☐ . ☐

The point of this reanalysis is simple. It checks to see if you express blocking equally in the three modalities. Here's how to interpret your kind of imbalance, if any:

1. *Relatively high score on COSB*: This third most common form of imbalance suggests something positive; you may be unusually good about letting others know you're blocking. But, on the other hand, you may not be fully in touch with internal aspects of blocking such as your self-talk and your feelings.

2. *Relatively high score on CCB*: This second most common form of imbalance has its pluses, notably the possibility that you are already aware of internal events that help block you. It also suggests that you may need to be more open in complaining about blocks.

3. *Relatively high score on SSSW*: This far and away most common form of imbalance points out an ignored factor in blocking. Many blockers are too private about their writing, too reluctant to impose on friends for help with writing, and too unsociable in establishing professional connections that help ensure success in writ-

ing. A disproportionately high score here, then, means that your blocking may be especially affected in this common way.

Component scores. Finally, you can identify specific components in your blocking by summing scores across the three questionnaires and entering their means/averages here:

1. work apprehension .... |___ __ . __|

2. procrastination .... |___ __ . __|

3. writing apprehension .... |___ __ . __|

4. dysphoria .... |___ __ . __|

5. impatience .... |___ __ . __|

6. perfectionism......................... |___ __ . __|

7. rules .... |___ __ . __|

If you've calculated correctly, the entered scores should fall in a range of 0 - 10. Preliminary samples of professionals seeking help for blocking and related writing problems produced these norms:

item(s)	median score
#1	6.8
#2-6	5.5
#7	4.4

So, if your score falls below the median, or norm, of other blockers, you score below average for that blocking component. A profile chart makes the task easier. Simply reenter your component scores here:

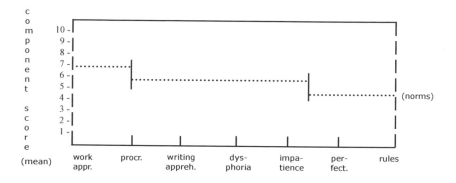

Then connect the points with a line to provide a profile of your scores.

This profile can be an important basis of comparison in the long run. Ideally, your profile then should be lower and more uniform. If it isn't, perhaps critical changes in behaving, thinking, feeling, and socializing as a writer need to be made.

Then, as now, it will help to know something about the nature of the components, of how each acts to block, and what high scores mean.

Application

1. **Work apprehension:** This most popular accompaniment of blocking necessitates a reminder of something writers have all heard elsewhere: correlation doesn't prove causation. In fact, work apprehension is also typical among people who already write with apparent ease. Most people, even unblocked people, like to complain about writing and suppose that it is unnaturally hard work.

If work apprehension doesn't really help identify blockers, why pay attention to it? Because it probably does in fact contribute to blocking by making writing seem so difficult and unreasonable. And because a goal in helping blocked (and unblocked) writers is to get them to the point where writing is painless, even enjoyable–the ultimate criterion of unblocking.

You can live with a high work apprehension score. It alone probably won't keep you blocked. But, you don't need to.

2. *Procrastination:* This is a vital factor in blocking. It blocks in ways already familiar, by putting off writing so that it either a) doesn't get done at all, or b) gets delayed until the writing cannot be done well or comfortably. Procrastination also works in more subtle and undermining ways. Procrastinators seek help for their "bad habits," they're good at enlisting the aid of concerned others, but then they tend to reject or undermine that help.

This means that a high score in procrastination requires special efforts to work at two levels–first, at managing your time more effectively; second, at monitoring temptations to feel you're being forced to do something you don't want to do.

When I work directly with procrastinators, I say something like this:

- "Look, I know you're uncomfortable. You're probably feeling that I'm taking too much control, that you're not sure you want to do this. But let's be sure we're in touch with something else: First, all we're talking about is changing your habits related to writing, not your whole lifestyle. Second, what we're doing relates to the very thing you've already admitted you want help with–not getting enough writing done."

3. *Writing apprehension:* A high score here means that nervousness and fearfulness get in the way of writing. Writing apprehension blocks just as surely and as commonly as does procrastination. It works via fears of failure and public embarrassment, and with less identifiable sources of anxiety that can even produce panic.

Writing apprehension, despite its pervasive role in blocking, offers excellent prospects for improvement. Consider its parallel to a more familiar form of apprehension, public speaking anxiety. In both cases, sufferers benefit mainly from exposure–getting in there and discovering that it's not as bad as imagined–and from developing the confidence associated with learning ways of transforming anxiety into enthusiastic, competent performances.

4. *Dysphoria:* A high score here means that problems of well-being are contributing to blocking. Writers are the best judges of how situational or how chronic the problem is. When it's chronic, with severe depression or suspiciousness that others are deliberately undermining their attempts, writers should seek professional help.

In my experience, simple dysphoria usually improves dramatically when writing is regular and successful and when the writer feels more competent. But, I've never seen a case of chronic depression or of debilitating problems such as phobias or suspiciousness that didn't necessitate direct, thorough going contact with a mental health professional.

5. *Impatience:* This blocking component resembles work apprehension (except that it is less common): Writers can live with it; many successful writers do. But writers don't need to.

Impatience helps block via a sense of urgency: not enough prewriting gets done (e.g., note taking, reflection, conceptual outlining) to permit the preparation that good writing demands; not enough rewriting or proofing is done to convey the writing in polished, error-free form; not enough writing gets done in comfortable, non-fatiguing fashion.

In severe form, impatience disrupts writing by making writers obsess about being hopelessly behind, feeling incapable of working fast enough or well enough to even bother trying. It does something else equally problematic: it turns into annoyance with the perceived slowness, even incompetence, of others who aren't so caught up in hurrying. People who might have helped–editors, colleagues, spouses–eventually try to avoid impatient writers because criticism, however well-intentioned, gets perceived as envy or persecution. Prognosis for working with impatience is mixed. Improvement, in my experience, depends in part on a willingness to learn new habits of writing (e.g., working in regular, but moderate sessions), of tolerating temporary incompleteness and slow but steady productivity, and of interacting constructively with audiences including significant others and editors. Still, some writers, perhaps because they are constitutionally A-types,[4] show moderate change in impatience while excelling at all other aspects of a writing program.

6. *Perfectionism:* Internal critics provide most of the demand for maladaptive perfectionism. Its source, like most internal voices that tell us what to do for our own good, can be traced to authority figures, especially teachers and mentors.

Perfectionism blocks when it occurs too early in the writing process, while the writer is preparing or still generating preliminary drafts. Perfectionism, with some limits, works to advantage in refining the last draft and in proofreading. Used prior to that, however, it disrupts momentum (e.g., when stopping to check accuracy), it demands too much to be managed reasonably, and it disheartens by reminding writers that they should strive for originality, greatness, perfection (of course), and similarly irrational goals while beginning a project.

The prognosis, here again, is mixed. A few writers, in my experience, refuse to abandon their maladaptive styles of perfectionism, supposing that doing so is tantamount to abandoning civilized standards of excellence. In this regard, perfectionism resembles shyness[5] in that its possessors tend to be nice people who are closet elitists.

Perfectionists can learn to laugh at their perfectionism and to put it in its proper place—toward the end of the writing process. They do so, at least in the short run, by confronting their internal critic and by writing around him or her.

7. *Rules:* This relatively uncommon component can be just as troublesome as any other. As its name implies, it involves rigid ways of dealing with writing, ways difficult to abandon until shown maladaptive. Rules interfere with efficient, painless writing when they incorporate an unfailing refusal to, say, outline. And they interrupt when their rigidity conflicts with the inherent demands of writing for flexible, recursive approaches.[6]

Maladaptive rules, in my experience, offer the best prognosis of the seven blocking components. Once demonstrated to be inefficient and unnecessary, they are eventually abandoned by all but a few writers.

Notes

[1] Daly, J. A. (1985). Writing apprehension. In M. Rose (Ed.), *When a writer can't write*. New York: Guilford.

[2] Daly, J. A., & Miller, M. D. (1975). The empirical development of an instrument to measure writing apprehension. *Research in the Teaching of English, 9*, 242-249.

[3] Boice, R. (1985). Cognitive components of blocking. *Written Communication, 2*, 91-104.

[4] Friedman, M., & Rosenman, R. H. (1974). *Type A behavior and your heart*. Greenwich, CT: Fawcett Crest.

[5] Zimbardo, P. G. (1977). *Shyness*. New York: Jove/HBJ.

[6] Rose, M. (1984). *Writer's block: The cognitive dimension*. Edwardsville, IL: Southern Illinois University Press.

Part Two:

An Annotated Bibliography on Blocking and Other Hindrances to Writing

Abstract

ONE HUNDRED critical summaries of examples from the literature on writing blocks were arbitrarily selected to convey a sense of early views of blocking (e.g., Freud's warning about internal critics), of contemporary curatives (e.g., cognitive therapies that purport to change a writer's inhibitory self- talk), of successful writers' accounts of past blocking (e.g., Joan Didion's recollection of feeling she had suffered a small aphasic stroke), of scientific assessments of writing problems (e.g., Daly and Miller's Writing Apprehension Scale), of differences in conceptualizing and treating blocks (e.g., psychoanalytic vs. behavioral), and of ways by which writing can be made less painful for all writers. Taken together, these sources provide a broad view of blocking and of the composing process, one that may suggest more eclectic approaches to the study of writing. Moreover, this diverse literature provides fascinating reading that has proven effective as bibliotherapy.

More specifically, this annotated bibliography suggests several distinctive patterns in an emerging psychology of writing. The first concerns the evolution of treatment strategies. In its initial form, help for writers revolved around automaticity–writing quickly, unselfconsciously, and uncritically. This treatment persists as the single-most popular antidote for blocking, and what was once known as automatic writing is now called free writing. Next came external controls. As psychology became more behavioral, so did its curatives. Typical programs for writers entailed time-management scheduling and contingency management, the former helping writers find time for writing, the latter pushing them to work regardless of mood.

The next stage was more recent, drawing on the trend to cognitive therapies. Increasingly, writing block treatments incorporate cognitive and emotional reeducation. The final stage grew from feminist concerns about the exclusion of some aspiring writers from the "old boy network" of advice and support in finding ideas, resources, and outlets for writing. Outgrowths of this movement include programs that help writers make their writing more public (e.g., collaborative) and more publicly acceptable (e.g., writing with a useful sense of audience).

Another pattern discernable in these annotations concerns the traditional controversies over the nature of writing, arguments which have inhibited progress in seeing writing as an understandable and treatable set of phenomena. Briefly, these bipolarities include questions as to 1) whether good writing should be spontaneous or produced/forced; 2) whether writing can be taught or if it can, at best, be learned; 3) whether writing treatments are best done rationally or irrationally; and 4) whether the act of writing is inherently healthy or pathological.

The final pattern that emerges from this literature is an increase in empirical and systematic studies. We are, at last, beginning to understand what predisposes some writers to blocking and what helps them unblock.

An Annotated Bibliography on Blocking and Other Hindrances to Writing

The literature on writing blocks has accumulated in diverse places. Its authors often show little awareness of precedents and parallels to their own studies and musings. But the pity of that neglect goes beyond formal scholarship; much of this literature makes for fascinating and useful reading.

I selected the 100 examples that follow to display the evolution, the heterogeneity, and the landmarks in experiential accounts and in research about blocking. Inclusion does not necessarily speak to excellence, but more likely to representation of a genre (e.g., art psychotherapy; humor), to perspectives on causes and types of blocking (e.g., fear of failure), to curatives (e.g., writing before editing), or to research in related areas (e.g., test anxiety; procrastination).

1. Adams, J. L. (1978). *Conceptual blockbusting*. New York: W. W. Norton.
    This popularized book on creative blocks reviews rituals writers use to ensure productivity (e.g., Schiller's desk with rotten apples) and psychological speculations about creativity (e.g., a creative person is sensitive to both the needs and limitations of his/her unconscious). Given this overview, Adams proposes five kinds of "emotional" blocks: a) fear of mistakes, b) distaste for chaos, c) judging rather than generating ideas, d) inability to incubate ideas, and e) excessive or minimal levels of motivation.
2. Amabile, T. M. (1985). Motivation and creativity: Effects of motivational orientation on creative writers. *Journal of Personality and Social Psychology, 48*, 393-399.
    Amabile promotes the popular notion that extrinsic motivation produces less creativity in writing than does intrinsic motivation. Her undergraduate subjects produced two simple poems, the first spontaneously, the second after they had rank-ordered their motives for writing from either an intrinsically or extrinsically oriented list. Subjects exposed to the list of intrinsic reasons produced poems that were subjectively rated as more creative than poems by the group exposed to the extrinsic list. Amabile concludes that mere exposure to extrinsic motives can inhibit creativity in writing.
3. Anonymous (1977). Beating writer's block. *Time, 110*(8), 101.
    An unusually good example of humor about blocking, this article chronicles the self-talk accompanying a block. Tactic number one is remembering bromides about blocking:

    > 9:25 a.m. (*Try to beat the block by leading off with other people's quotes.*) "Blocks are simply forms of egotism," said Lawrence Durrell.

    Tactic number two is facing the aggressive realities of trying to write for publication: "Herman Melville was so wounded by critics that he wrote no fiction at all for thirty years."

    > 12:15 a.m. (word count so far: 385) Short break for inner movie about receiving Nobel Prize for literature. (p. 101)
4. Asimov, I. (1979, 1980). *In memory yet green; In joy still felt*. New York: Avon.
    Isaac Asimov, a most prolific writer, contradicts the usual recommendations of writing teachers; he rarely revises, he deletes transition passages. In these first two volumes of his autobiography,

Asimov lists ways to avoid trouble in starting (by beginning as late in the script as practical), to develop a sense of audience, and to avoid blocking:

> "What if you get a writer's block?" (That's a favorite question.) I say, "I don't ever get one precisely because I switch from one task to another at will. If I'm tired of one project, I just switch to something else which, at that moment, interests me more." (p. 192, IJSF)

5. Barrios, M. V., & Singer, J. L. (1981). The treatment of creative blocks: A comparison of waking imagery, hypnotic dream, and rational discussion techniques. *Imagination, Cognition, and Personality, 1,* 89-109.

   Forty subjects with creative blocks were exposed to one of four quasi-experimental groups: waking imagery, hypnotically induced dream imagery, rational discussions, and a non-treatment control. Although subjects worked systematically (e.g., imaginal sessions), Barrios and Singer provide only vague accounts of their results. Apparently, subjects with waking or hypnotically induced imagery unblocked more readily than subjects in the other two groups. An interesting sidelight about the possible role of mental imagery in blocking: subjects with lower levels of guilty or hostile daydreaming at pretreatment were more likely to unblock during treatment.

6. Beck, A. T., Rush, J. A., Shaw, B. F., & Emery, G. (1979). *Cognitive therapy of depression.* New York: Guilford.

   This most readable and useful account of behavioral-cognitive therapies begins with the premise that distressed people are susceptible to kinds of distorted thinking that set up a vicious cycle. Depression leads to a reduced level of activity, which leads to labeling oneself as ineffectual, which leads to further discouragement and immobility—and so on—including increasing passivity and social isolation. The applicability of this approach to blockers is especially evident in advice to writers such as this: Remind yourself that trying to carry out plans is an important first step.

7. Bergler, E. (1950). Does "writer's block" exist? *American Imago, 7,* 43-54.

   As if to illustrate his earlier contention in *The Writer and Psychoanalysis* (1950) that writers are necessarily neurotic, Bergler launches an emotional attack against the "fallacious arguments" of "naive contemporaries" who criticized his book.

8. Bergler, E. (1950). *The writer and psychoanalysis.* Garden City, NY: Doubleday.

    Bergler, an enormously productive writer on psychoanalytic topics, offers a curious view of "writing blocks" (the term he claims to have invented). He supposes that a) all writers are neurotic (writing is an oral regression and so is linked to homosexuality and alcoholism); b) all writers write in hope of self-engendered cure; and c) writers block when they, in effect, reject their mothers by unconsciously refusing to write as a substitute for rejecting their mothers' milk. Unfortunately, Bergler communicates disgust for writers and a suspicion that, if successfully psychoanalyzed, many would recognize the wisdom in abandoning writing. Still, Bergler's extensive experience with blockers yields a number of useful insights such as this: Writers too often are motivated by an unhealthy need to indulge in "injustice collecting" (p. 262).

9. Bergler, E. (1955). Unconscious mechanisms in "writer's block." *Psychoanalytic Review, 42,* 160-168.

    In this follow-up to his *The Writer and Psychoanalysis* (1950), Bergler presents more studied defenses of his work in terms of its substantial basis ("on *clinical* analysis of more than 40 writers") and in outlining the four main hurdles to unblocking (e.g., scopophilia–a conflict between exhibitionism and voyeurism). Bergler is especially direct regarding treatment-outcome prospects with blockers: It is possible to remove the block in approximately 8 months" (p. 164).

10. Block, L. (1984). Overcoming the ultimate writer's block. *Writer's Digest, 64,* 20-24.

    Block writes humorously to make a basic point about what blocks fiction writers: negative beliefs (e.g., "I don't have enough talent") can turn into self-fulfilling prophecies. Block's article is a rare treatment of blocking in the popularized literature for aspiring writers.

11. Bloom, L. Z. (1981, March). *Why graduate students can't write: Implications of research on writing anxiety for graduate education.* Paper presented at the Conference on College Composition and Communication, Dallas.

    Bloom posits a relatively unique agent of blocking as a major cause of writing anxiety among graduate students: prior success in writing that may have come too readily or indiscriminately. She also discusses other blocking factors endemic to graduate school such as mixed social roles of independence and dependence, ambiguous assignments, and undermining spouses.

12. Bloom, L. Z. (1985). Anxious writers in context; Graduate school and beyond. In M. Rose (Ed.), *When writers can't write* (pp. 119-133). New York: Guilford.

Bloom, a veteran in conducting workshops for student and professional writers, presents two case studies of dissertation writers. She shows how writers, especially women, bring individualized differences in perception, ability, disposition, and external conditions to their tasks. Bloom's emphasis is on conflicts in those contexts that teachers and mentors might otherwise ignore and, in so doing, help exacerbate into blocking.

13. Boice, R. (1982). Increasing the writing productivity of 'blocked' academicians. *Behaviour Research & Therapy, 20*, 197- 207.

Six blocked academicians were exposed to experimental paradigms, at least a year in length, where contracted external contingencies (i.e., pressures) helped induce unblocking and quantitative evidence of regular productivity in scholarly writing. The therapeutic approach used with blockers is described in terms of three stages that precede contingency management: 1) self-monitoring of writing habits and distractions; 2) dealing with resistance to help via techniques such as free/automatic writing; and 3) use of social support for writing by, for example, arranging the aid of colleagues and students in observing undisrupted writing times.

14. Boice, R. (1983). Contingency management in writing and the appearance of creative ideas: Implications for the treatment of writing blocks. *Behaviour Research & Therapy, 21*, 537-543.

A commonly stated resistance to entering programs for blocking inspired this article: Many people assume that writing forced by external pressures must be lacking in creativity. This experiment with 27 blocked academicians showed, in contrast to that view, that . . .

> Contingency management of writing productivity seems to facilitate, not impede, the appearance of creative ideas for writing. That is, subjects who were "forced" to write by a powerful external contingency not only produced more written copy but also generated more creative ideas for writing than did subjects who wrote spontaneously. Subjects who

were encouraged to write more but who were not pressured to do so with contingencies reported moderate levels of creative ideas. And subjects who voluntarily refrained from writing had minimal levels of logged creativity. (pp. 540-541)

15. Boice, R. (1983). Experimental and clinical treatments of writing blocks. *Journal of Consulting and Clinical Psychology, 51*, 183-191.

How important is the therapist in effecting unblocking? This experimental study of unblocking in two matched groups of academicians with writing blocks suggests that the techniques may be more critical than the person administering them. The group that had minimal personal contact in carrying out an unblocking program based around techniques of contingency management showed the same levels of writing output as did the group with individual weekly therapy sessions plus the same techniques. And, as in previous research (Boice, 1982), the experimental manipulations indicated that one thing, contingency management, helped initiate and maintain writing far more effectively than others.

16. Boice, R. (1984). Reexamination of traditional emphases in faculty development. *Research in Higher Education, 21*, 195-209.

Thirty-two faculty exposed to lengthy behavioral programs for unblocking not only showed regular and persistent success in completing and publishing manuscripts, but also evidenced parallel improvement in dimensions including collegiality, classroom performance, and burnout. Thus, some common excuses for not writing—that it necessarily interferes with teaching, with social life, and with general well-being—are contradicted by the data collected in this project.

17. Boice, R. (1985). Cognitive components of blocking. *Written Communication, 2*, 91-104.

Sixty subjects, 40 of them blockers, provided over 5,000 examples of self-talk accompanying the initiation and completion of writing sessions. An inductive procedure of sorting those thought-list cards into reliable and discrete categories produced seven cognitive components of blocking (listed in descending order of importance): 1) work apprehension, 2) procrastination, 3) dysphoria, 4) impatience, 5) perfectionism, 6) evaluation anxiety, and 7) rigid rules. Blockers were more likely than nonblockers to list negative thoughts and less likely to evidence "psych-up" thoughts during writing sessions.

18. Boice, R. (1985). Psychotherapies for writing blocks. In M. Rose (Ed.), *When a writer can't write* (pp. 182-218). New York: Guilford. This review of psychological approaches to blocking offers two relatively unique approaches to unblocking: 1) descriptions of psychoanalytically oriented therapies, specifically using the theory and methods of Eric Erikson: "What makes Erikson's approach more contemporary is his emphasis on endowing the ego with qualities including trust and hope, autonomy and will, industry and competence, generativity and care" (p. 8); and, 2) a review of the literature on free writing/automatic writing with an experimental demonstration of its efficacy in unblocking.

19. Boice, R. (1989). Procrastination, busyness, and bingeing. *Behaviour Research & Therapy.*
The first inquiry employed repeated surveys and direct observations to show that procrastinators are unreliable reporters of how they spend their time. The second inquiry tested an intervention for procrastination (i.e., helping new faculty find brief, daily sessions in which to write). Overall, the study confirmed the notion that procrastination, at least for a relatively unstructured task like scholarly writing, has at least two central components: bingeing and busyness.

20. Boice, R., & Johnson, K. (1984). Perception and practice of writing for publication at a doctoral-granting university. *Research in Higher Education, 21*, 33-43.
This survey of 685 faculty on a campus where writing for publication is valued highly indicates a preponderance of questionable habits (e.g., writing mostly in binges just before deadlines), a moderate level of functionally discouraging experiences with the editorial process, and a low but still significant level of blocking (12%).

21. Boice, R., & Jones, F. (1984). Why academicians don't write. *Journal of Higher Education, 55*, 567-582.
The emphases of this review of factors that make writing for publication difficult are: 1) writing is an essential educational experience for teachers that can facilitate development in related areas such as teaching; 2) part of what keeps many prospective writers from writing is traditional mysticism about writing such as the belief that it should be spontaneous, original, and perfect; and 3) another powerful deterrent is an often undemocratic, inhumane editorial process.

22. Boice, R., & Myers, P. E. (1986). Two parallel traditions: automatic writing and free writing. *Written Communication, 3*, 471-490.
    Automaticity, effortless writing that comes with freedom from excessive conscious interference, is reviewed in terms of its origins in automatic writing (e.g., spiritism) and its growth into contemporary techniques such as free writing. Boice and Myers characterize automaticity as dissociation from consciousness, as aids to spontaneity/creativity, and as aids to unblocking.

23. Boudin, H. M. (1972). Contingency contracting as a therapeutic tool in the deceleration of amphetamine use. *Behavior Therapy, 3*, 604-608.
    The subject of this single-case study felt unable to complete her research report without amphetamines. The therapist, using techniques of dubious ethicality, had the subject stay in his home where she earned food, liquor, cigarettes, and a favorite sleeping location by completing typed pages. The techniques evidently worked.

24. Bowers, P. (1979). Hypnosis and creativity: The search for the missing link. *Journal of Abnormal Psychology, 88*, 564-572.
    Bowers explores a concept of great potential importance to understanding blocking, hypnotizability. Her research with students and writers in contexts of storytelling and writing under hypnosis suggests that "high hypnotizables" bring several advantages to creative tasks: 1) they select information in ways that stimulate fantasy, 2) they give imaginative responses more easily, and 3) they let imaginative experiences carry them along unselfconsciously. In other words, "high hypnotizables" write effortlessly, whereas "low hypnotizables" tend to struggle with volitional, effortful means of trying to remain in control of the process. Presumably, although Bowers does not speak directly to this issue, an overly volitional, effortful mode of writing could engender blocking and interfere with the "right-brained" methods typically used for unblocking.

25. Brande, D. (1934). *Becoming a writer*. New York: Harcourt Brace.
    This recently reprinted classic offers simple, direct writing: "First there is the difficulty of writing *at all*. The full, abundant flow that must be established ... simply will not begin." It offers a clear accounting of writer's block, one that precedes Bergler's (1950) claim to precedence. And it offers a prescription for what Elbow (1973)

later called free writing as a curative for blocking. The point of practicing effortless writing, Brande notes, is being able to write at any given time: "to teach yourself that no excuse of any nature can be offered when the moment comes."

26. Brian, M., Augusto, F., & Wilson, G. T. (1981). In vivo exposure vs. cognitive restructuring in the treatment of scriptophobia. *Behaviour Research & Therapy, 19*, 525-532.

An example of the small literature on phobias about writing in public, this article distinguishes scriptophobia from simple phobias like fear of heights:

> Whereas with a simple phobia the avoidance and the fear are both relatively circumscribed, with scriptophobia the fear is much broader than a simple fear of writing. What seems to underlie the fear of writing is a more general social apprehensiveness, of which fear is only one manifestation. (p. 531)

27. Cowley, M. (1978). *–And I worked at the writer's trade*. New York: Viking Press.

Cowley edited *The Paris Review Interviews* (1958), a classic series of interviews with famous writers. He reprints the introduction to that series in this book, a reminiscence of a brilliant literary career. Taken together, the anecdotes from the *Interviews* selected by Cowley provide a unique sense of how writers write and of how they forestall blocking:

> Apparently the hardest problem for almost any writer, whatever his medium, is getting to work in the morning (or in the after noon, if he is a late riser like Styron, or even at night). Thornton Wilder says, "Many writers have told me that they have built up mnemonic devices to start them off on each day's writing task ... My springboard has always been long walks." (pp. 188- 189)

28. Daly, J. A. (1985). Writing apprehension. In M. Rose (Ed.), *When a writer can't write* (pp. 43-82). New York: Guilford.

The problem with most information about blocking, Daly notes at the outset, is its basis in anecdotes; systematic investigations of writers' feelings about writing are all too recent. Daly's own work on writing apprehension helps correct that traditional oversight by providing a) a reliable and valid questionnaire to assess apprehension, b) a heterogeneous sample of writers and of correlations between apprehension and factors such as self-esteem (writing apprehension is specific to writing) or careers demanding much writing, c) a system of nine interrelated explanations for writing apprehension (e.g., perceptions of writing teachers as sources of punishment), and d) educational/ therapeutic programs to alleviate writing apprehension. Daly concludes that types of dispositional attitudes must be matched to appropriate treatments; thus, "real" blocking requires remediation with free writing, whereas procrastination is best treated via time management.

29. Daly, J. A., & Miller, M. D. (1975). The empirical development of an instrument to measure writing apprehension. *Research in the Teaching of English, 9,* 242-249.

In a landmark article detailing the development of the objective measure of behaviors, emotions, and cognitions related to blocking, Daly and Miller provide a questionnaire, a self report device modeled after assessments of speech anxiety, to assess writing apprehension. Its general categories include anxiety about writing in general and experiences with teachers' evaluations. Its 26 items, selected via factor analysis, include "1) I avoid writing, 2) I have no fear of my writing being evaluated, 19) I like seeing my thoughts on paper, 26) I'm no good at writing."

30. Didion, Joan. (1981). *Slouching towards Bethlehem*. New York: Washington Square Press.

This successful novelist provides an unusually candid account of blocking:

> I went to San Francisco because I had not been able to work in some months, had been paralyzed with the conviction that writing was an irrelevant act (p. 11). . . There is always a point in the writing of a piece when I sit in a room literally papered with false starts and cannot put one word after another and imagine that I have suffered a small stroke, leaving me apparently undamaged but actually aphasic. (p. 13).

31. Dillon, M. J., & Malott, R. W. (1981). Supervising masters theses and doctoral dissertations. *Teaching of Psychology, 8,* 195-201.

Dillon and Malott facilitated almost every aspect of getting students through theses and dissertations, from generating literature reviews to eliciting effective guidance from mentors. Their behavioral program emphasized task-descriptions (i.e., goal setting), performance guidelines (e.g., directives on reading journal articles), and a powerful contingency.

32. Dillon, M. J., Kent, H. M., & Malott, R. W. (1980). A supervisory system for accomplishing long-range projects: An application to master's thesis research. *Journal of Organizational Behavior Management, 2*, 213-227.

    Evidently the first experimental study of unblocking with more than a single subject, this article describes a system for overcoming procrastination with five behavioral techniques: 1) written task specification, 2) weekly sub-goals or deadlines, 3) weekly monitoring of work habits, 4) weekly feedback from faculty supervisors on the quality of work completed, and 5) added incentives of losing pre-specified amounts of money for failures to meet deadlines. Task completion was higher for the 15 master's level students when feedback was in effect (91%) than otherwise (65%).

33. Domash, L. (1976). The therapeutic use of writing in the service of the ego. *Journal of the American Academy of Psychoanalysis, 4*, 261-269.

    This example from a modest literature based around therapies in which patients express themselves via writing has some relevance to blocking: that is, therapeutic writing seems to give patients more control over potentially overwhelming impulses, including a reluctance to write.

34. Downey, J. E. (1918). A program for a psychology of literature. *Journal of Applied Psychology, 2*, 366-377.

    This forgotten paper outlines ways of understanding and enhancing writing skills with attention to processes such as mental imagery, inner speech, rhythm, and literary empathy. Downey suggests interesting distinctions between writers (e.g., prosaic vs. poetic types) and methods of increasing literary productivity (e.g., development of observational skills vs. suspended inhibitions). While she does not mention blocking explicitly, Downey mentions two related problems, lack of momentum and mental laziness. Her solutions for inhibited writing include these: "Think into your typewriter" and "never stop at the end" (p. 375).

35. Edwards, B. (1979). *Drawing on the right side of the brain*. Los Angeles: J. P. Tarcher.

    One of the most potentially useful sources of help for blockers is not about writing at all. Betty Edwards' bestseller on learning to draw realistically and painlessly uses techniques that can work as nicely with writing. She outlines ways of learning how to visualize things accurately, of acquiring calm confidence in creative abilities, and of utilizing the spatial, relational aspects of the mind.

36-37. Elbow, P. (1973). *Writing without teachers*. New York: Oxford University Press.

Elbow's little book may rank foremost among helpful sources. His method of treating blocks, free writing, is neither original nor comprehensive. But it comprises the critical first step in getting unblocked and its presentation is convincing, even inspirational. Whatever else, Elbow knows how to induce momentum in writing.

Elbow's sequel to *Writing Without Teachers, Writing With Power* (Oxford: 1981), may fail in trying to do too much. *Power* is no less readable or interesting (e.g., an insight into why English teachers are so likely to block, p. 21), but its larger scheme of taking readers beyond free writing into more abstract skills like "voice" somehow loses its compellingness.

38. Flower, L. S., & Hayes, J. R. (1980). The cognition of discovery: Defining a rhetorical problem. *College Composition and Communication, 31*, 21-32.

This well-known paper emphasizes writing as a problem-solving, a cognitive process whereby the most crucial act is finding or defining the problem to be solved. Flower and Hayes' related insight about blocking is too easily overlooked: myths about the ease of discovering what needs to be said cause some writers to give up too soon.

39. Flower, L. S., & Hayes, J. R. (1984). Images, plans, and prose: The representation of meaning in writing. *Written Communication, 1*, 120-160.

Flower and Hayes organize the complexity of writing into simple points like this: A writer's knowledge may be stored as visual images, perceptual cues, and other mental representations of meaning that may be differentially difficult to capture in words. Their analysis of the difficulties in translating mental representations and plans into writing points out an obvious place for blocking: The actual shift from mentation to writing often brings hesitation, loss of fluency, and confusion.

40. Freud, S. (1900). *The interpretation of dreams* (A. A. Brill, 1913, Trans.). New York: Macmillan.

While Freud does not speak directly about writing blocks, he uses an insight from another literary giant, Schiller, to offer one of the best-known explanations of blocking: The first part describes how freely and self-consciously mental events flow when writing is successful: "In the case of a creative mind, however, the intelligence has withdrawn its watchers from the gates, the ideas rush in pell-mell and only then the great heap is looked over and critically examined." The second part is the famous allegory about a "watcher at the gates" and what happens when the "watcher" becomes an internal critic:

> You are ashamed or afraid of the momentary and transitory madness which is found in all real creators, and whose longer or shorter duration distinguishes the thinking artist from the dreamer... you reject too soon and discriminate too severely. (p. 80)

41. Friedman, M., & Rosenman, R. H. (1974). *Type A behavior and your heart.* Greenwich, CT: Fawcett Crest.

This landmark description of the type A personality (the coronary-prone individual who struggles incessantly, aggressively to achieve more and more in less time) suggests a kinship to many blockers: unnecessary, self-imposed deadlines; quest for numbers or quantity (often while procrastinating); inability to accept praise or to praise oneself; belief that there must be time enough to do all important things; and a sense of persecution.

42. Galbraith, D. (1980). The effect of conflicting goals on writing: A case study. *Visible Language, 14,* 364-375.

Evidently the first published account of treating a blocked writer by a composition teacher, this report of a single subject who postponed and interrupted her writing describes cumulative stages of treatment which produced dramatic success, evidently because once in motion, the subject found that a) writing alleviated writing anxiety, and b) themes and structure emerged spontaneously.

43. Gardner, J. (1983). *On becoming a novelist.* New York: Harper Colophon.

Gardner, a successful novelist (e.g., *October Light*) and veteran teacher of creative writing, pays especial attention to the things that often inhibit writing, including blocking: "In his non-inspired state, the writer feels all the world to be mechanical, made up of numbered separate parts: he does not see wholes but particulars, not spirit but matter" (pp. 119-120). With all his insight and experience, Gardner might be expected to offer some great solutions for blocking. Not so. He evidently believes that blocking depends on forces beyond our control.

44. Goodman, P. (1952) On writer's block. *Complex, 7*, 42-50.
    Inhibited authors, Goodman concludes, are deficient in dissociating their writing from their own actuality. The blocked writer, then, becomes so rigidly bound up with his interpersonal situation that he or she cannot play while writing. Every detail seems relevant; the writing becomes overburdened.

45. Graves, D. (1985). Blocking and the young writer. In M. Rose (Ed.), *When a writer can't write* (pp. 1-18). New York: Guilford.
    Graves, a direct observer of elementary school writers, concludes that children focus on the concerns of the moment and so can get stuck on them. Further, their teachers and parents often do little more than stress the mechanical components of writing in trying to help children; the result of instruction from people with little experience in topic choice or rethinking of information can be a lifetime block in composing. Children, for example, may conclude they have little to say because they can't spell. The child simply says, "I don't know what to write about" (p. 17).

46. Haar, M. D., & Salovey, P. (1984). *The efficacy of cognitive-behavior and writing process training for alleviating writing anxiety.* Unpublished manuscript, Pacific Graduate School of Psychology, Menlo Park, CA.
    Fifty-one of the 91 subjects who responded to an advertisement for people with problems about avoiding writing met the standards for inclusion in this study by scoring above criterion level in the Writing Apprehension Test (Daly and Miller, 1975) and on both the Writing Anxiety and the Writing Block subscales of the Writing Problem Profile. They participated in groups with a) cognitive-behavior therapy (i.e., countering negative self-talk about writing) combined with writing process instruction (e.g., free writing); b) writing process instruction alone; or c) no-treatment. Results: "Only the combination treatment resulted in significant improvement on a performance measure, writing quality" (p. 2).

47. Hall, B. L., & Hursch, D. E. (1982). An evaluation of the effects of a time management program on work efficiency. *Journal of Organizational Behavior Management, 3,* 73-96.

    This article provides a thorough review of the literature and research on procrastination (conclusion: there are lots of recommendations for curing procrastination but no data to support them) and a study of four faculty members who had been unable to complete writing tasks on time. Hall and Hursch had their faculty subjects work toward greater emphasis on high priority work by setting up and posting activity schedules and by breaking long-term goals into manageable tasks. Only one of the four subjects failed to manage consistent productivity on important tasks, but even he showed greater efficiency overall.

48. Harris, M. B. (1974). Accelerating dissertation writing: A case study. *Psychological Reports, 34,* 984-986.

    This successful replication of Nurnberger and Zimmerman's (1970) "productive avoidance technique" helped a procrastinating student finish her dissertation on schedule.

49. Hatterer, L. J. (1965). *The artist in society: Problems and treatment of the creative personality.* New York: Grove Press.

    Hatterer discusses multiple causes of blocking in terms of emotional disorders (e.g., depression and withdrawal, hostility, bizarre sexual practices), ritualistic work habits, realistic fears of the lonely drudgery required for creative work, and, for women, the birth of a child. But his prescriptions are vague (e.g., "be patient, listen to his plans for work, and meet his demands for reassurance") and sometimes questionable ("It is best for the artist not to discuss his block with others" (p. 136)).

50. Henning, L. H. (1981). Paradox as a treatment for writer's block. *Personnel and Guidance Journal, 60,* 112-113.

    Henning's article is a paradoxically rare contribution on blocking from counseling and educational psychology, a field that specializes in helping students with related problems such as test anxiety. The paradox in the title refers to a therapeutic technique whereby the therapist encourages the patient to engage in the undesired behavior while disguising longer-term motives of the therapy. In this vague report of a cure, Henning provoked a single subject to write by encouraging him to deliberately produce the poor, mistake-rid-den copy he so feared. So it was, evidently, that the writer unwittingly overcame his over-perfectionism and began writing regularly.

51. Hinsie, L. E., & Campbell, R. J. (1974). *Psychiatric dictionary* (4th ed.). New York: Oxford University Press.

     Psychiatrists, beginning perhaps with Bleuler's nineteenth-century observation that schizophrenics show blocking in speech patterns, have developed the general notion of blocking as a symptom of psychopathology. This example of a contemporary definition shows how the concept has broadened from its earlier usages in ways that suggest relevance to some blocked writers:

     > *block, affect* Inability to discharge emotions adequately or appropriately, seen typically in obsessive-compulsives, who often appear cold, unfeeling and emotionally stiff and over controlled, and also in some schizophrenics... (p. 99)

52. Hull, G. A. (1981). Effects of self-management strategies on journal writing by college freshmen. *Research in the Teaching of English, 15*, 135-148.

     Hull reports experiments with beginning college writers that indicate the efficacy of two behavioral techniques, self-monitoring and goal-setting, in raising the frequency and amounts of journal writing. Her emphasis, one overlooked by many composition teachers, was "not on inducing writing as a school performance, but on establishing a writing habit outside the classroom" (p. 137).

53. Jensen, G. H., & DiTiberio, J. K. (1983, Spring). The MBTI and writing blocks. *MBTI News, 14-15.*

     MBTI stands for the Myers-Briggs Type Indicator, a personality inventory based around Carl Jung's notions of personality types. Jensen and DiTiberio use the MBTI to build a speculative but intriguing typology of personality styles and blocking tendencies. Summarized briefly, their system looks like this: *Extraverts* need "outer" activities such as oral presentations to avoid blocking; *Introverts* may block when they try to mentally plan the complete paper before beginning; *Sensing* types need specific and detailed instructions to write; *Intuitive* types get into difficulty when their style of letting one idea trigger another escalates into overly complex manuscripts; *Thinking* types overdevelop clear systems of presentation to the point where many readers see the writing as little more than an outline; *Feeling* types, in contrast, get so concerned with audience reactions that they block when unable to conjure up the perfect word or phrase to capture an inner value; *Judging* types may write before they have collected enough information to establish workable plans and goals; and *Perceiving* types cast plans in so broad a fashion that they block upon realizing that they may never finish. The best way to avoid blocking, according to Jensen and DiTiberio, is to avoid being locked into the extremes of any one MBTI dimension.

54. Jones, A. C. (1975). Grandiosity blocks writing projects. *Transactional Analysis, 5*, 415.

This brief, anecdotal account of blocking is unusually substantive. Jones begins with a clear sense of blocking in terms of grandiosity:

> The erstwhile writer may cure him or herself by answering questions such as: "Am I expecting a masterful life work (perfection) when it is only a manageable one unit project?" "Do I have grandiose expectations of myself?" "Am I discounting my ability to do the job?" (p. 415)

Then, for a transactionalist, she sounds surprisingly like a behaviorist in specifying correctives:

> A person can usually move toward successful completion of a writing project after he defines success; that is, he states limits, goals, and steps within his capability. The person's making such a measurable description of the project rids him or her of the first and greatest hurdle to productional fluctuating definition of success. (p. 415)

55. Kronsky, B. J. (1979). Freeing the creative process: The relevance of Gestalt. *Art Psychotherapy, 6*, 233-240.

Kronsky is a gestalt psychotherapist (i.e., emphasizes "right-brain" prescriptions like "letting go" and "living in the moment") specializing in the little-known field of art psychotherapy. She uses her experience as a therapist to posit three causes of blocking: a) a holding attitude where the anxiety of grasping towards life becomes a worse problem than the anxiety it tries to avoid, b) negative self-attitudes, and c) fear of one's own energy and excitement. Solutions suggested by Kronsky include "grounding exercises" (i.e., becoming expert in trusting one's own impulses) and art exercises (e.g., automatic drawings).

56. Kubie, L. S. (1965, June). Blocks to creativity. *International Science & Technology*, 69-78.
    Kubie is an oft-cited author on blocking; he was one of the first writers to lend an aura of science to the topic. His speculation about why blocking occurs: creativity presumably depends on the free flow of preconscious material and is blocked when either the unconscious or conscious mind takes precedence. Kubie's solution to blocking: plan to work during times when the preconscious dominates (e.g., when tired) and to let solutions occur while sleeping. Later authors, armed with more systematic data (e.g., D. N. Perkins, *The mind's best work*, Harvard University Press, 1981), contest assumptions about the power of incubation as an engine for unblocking.

57. Lamberg, W. J. (1977). Major problems in doing academic writing. *College Composition and Communication, 28*, 26-29.
    Students attending workshops for writing problems produced a list of major difficulties in academic writing (e.g., lack of self-management skills, lack of strategy for the composing process, and difficulty with teachers' criticisms).

58. Levin, M. (1953). A new fear in writers. *Psychoanalysis, 2*, 34-38.
    A common fear of blockers, one rarely discussed in the literature, owes to doubts of knowing enough, of keeping up with developments in research. So it is, Levin concludes, that writers are more likely than other professionals to enter psychoanalysis. Another fear of blockers, one not often discussed by other authors, arises in the prospect of seeking therapeutic help: If one accepts the therapist as more expert regarding her/his own perceptions, what becomes of one's self-confidence as an artist?

59. Mack, K., & Skjei, E. (1979). *Overcoming writing blocks*. Los Angeles: J. P. Tarcher.
    Mack and Skjei provide the first, and to date, only comprehensive coverage of causes and treatments of blocking. Their book is thoroughgoing in describing the phenomenology of blocking ("You're paralyzed. You feel panicky, terrified, your mind is a blank," p. 15), in discussing reasons for blocking, and in prescribing a sequential process of unblocking in four stages: prewriting activities (e.g., minimizing distractions), organizing a conceptual framework (e.g., profiling a critical reader), writing rough drafts (e.g., a form

of free writing called "cooker sheets"), and revising (e.g., cut and paste). Curiously, Mack and Skjei insert disturbing messages that blockers may be weak and unable to help themselves: "mere self-discipline rarely works with a genuinely blocked writer, whose difficulty has recognizable emotional symptoms and some distinct psychological causes" (p. 23).

60. Meichenbaum, D., & Cameron, R. (1974). The clinical potential of modifying what clients say to themselves. In M. J. Mahoney & C. E. Thoresen (Eds.), *Self-control: Power to the person* (pp. 263-290). Monterey, CA: Brooks/Cole.

This landmark chapter on cognitive-behavioral treatments for test anxiety has broad application to blocking. Consider, for example, the three typical kinds of self-statements made by test-anxious subjects: a) they worry about their performance and about how others are doing; b) they ruminate over alternatives and denigrate the task at hand; and c) they obsess about feelings of inadequacy, about anticipated punishments, and about loss of esteem. Once test-anxious subjects are made aware of their negative self-statements, this approach teaches them to react by producing incompatible, creativity engendering statements (e.g., "I will defer judgments; I will invoke a no-stop rule; I will relax and let it happen").

61. Mellgren, A. (1976). Hypnosis and artistic concentration. *Journal of the American Society of Psychosomatic Dentistry and Medicine, 23*, 133-135.

Seventeen of Mellgren's dental patients complained of artistic blocking and of common anxieties, difficulties in concentrating, depression, and other working pains. When subjected to his hypnotic trance, each blocked artist was informed that: "after awakening, he would feel calmer, more self-confident, and would have received a certain inspiration" (p. 134). Three "established artists" then judged the resulting work and, in 13 of 17 cases, noted it superior to pre-hypnotic work. When three of the same subjects were later exposed to suggestions of failure, they either refused to pick up a pencil or threw it away.

62. Menks, F. (1979). Behavioral techniques in the treatment of a writing phobia. *American Journal of Occupational Therapy, 33*, 102-107.

This is a single-case study of a student who, prior to treatment, had experienced "panic and agitation when asked to write." Menks applied common palliatives for panic attacks–relaxation techniques that were administered before each of twenty writing sessions. Both kinds of records collected from the subject, of words written and doubting thoughts, showed appropriate changes.

63. Minninger, J. (1977). "Reteachering"-unlearning writing blocks. *Transactional Analysis, 7*, 71-72.

Minninger's accounts of how unblocking occurs illustrate the colorful language of transactional psychologists:

> Group members contract to leave their Critical Parents "down the hall"... As soon as the safety of the workshop situation is tested, most people shift from Adapted Child to Free Child... The author's Child invites their Child to play in a sandbox of words where no other Parent or Adult may enter. (p. 71)

In other words, Minninger got blockers to try free writing.

64. Murray, D. M. (1978). Write before writing. *College Composition and Communication, 29*, 375-381.

Murray, who champions prewriting exercises, offers advice that should help blockers (e.g., ideas come to a writer because s/he has a mind trained to seek them out). He also provides a memorable quote about inertia and blocking: "The negative force is *resistance* to writing, one of the great natural forces of nature. It may be called the Law of Delay: that writing which can be delayed, will be" (p. 375).

65. Newton, P. M. (1983). Periods in the adult development of the faculty member. *Human Relations, 36*, 441-458.

Newton deals with a neglected source of blocking, the predictable and painful stages of adult development. One troublesome period occurs around age 50, a time when failure to have completed the "work" of mid-life transition leads to chronic depression. Older academics in such a dilemma find nothing to maintain a sense of professional pride in their earlier work. They find no inner resources with which to develop in new directions. And they show symptoms of their immobilization in poor teaching and blocking.

66. Nurnberger, J. T., & Zimmerman, J. (1970). Applied analysis of human behavior: An alternative to conventional motivational inferences and unconscious determination in therapeutic programming. *Behavior Therapy, 1*, 59-60.

Apparently the first data-based study of unblocking, this article chronicles the behavioral treatment of an "ABD" professor unable to write for two years. Nurnberger and Zimmerman's premise is simple: neurotic behaviors including blocking are often maintained because they terminate, avoid, or postpone the anticipation of punishment. So, too, the treatment: the patient wrote out checks to a despised organization with the agreement that a check would be sent on each day that he did not reach his writing output goal. Not surprisingly, he wrote.

67. Oliver, L. J. (1982, November). Helping students overcome writer's block. *Journal of Reading*, 162-168.

This review for reading teachers teaches techniques to help students overcome blocking. The primary step, Oliver assumes, lies in determining if blockers subscribe to counterproductive rules and strategies in writing. Once dissuaded from their rigid rules (see Rose, 1980), students should then be stimulated, Oliver argues, via systematic questioning to generate new ideas for writing. Other techniques described here include free writing and paradoxical intention (i.e., "students can sometimes overcome blocking by trying to write badly," p. 167).

68. Osborne, A. (1983, February/March). Will micros eliminate "typing phobia?" *The Portable Companion*, 11.

Magazines for computer enthusiasts often contain brief articles such as this by Adam Osborne. He assumes that new developments in word processors will help remove phobias or blocks connected with writing; errors are now so easily corrected with a few "key strokes" that prospects of making mistakes no longer matter.

69. Passman, R. (1976). A procedure for eliminating writer's block in a college student. *Behavior Therapy & Experimental Psychiatry, 7*, 297-298.

Through the 1970s, articles in behavior therapy journals typically reported the results of a single patient and somewhat vague procedures—as in this study of a blocked college student who contracted to earn rewards by completing small segments of writing.

70. Pickering, G. (1974). *Creative malady*. New York: Delta.

A suspiciously select sample of anecdotes is used to support Pickering's hypothesis that the best writing is done by writers who are physically ill. Indeed, Pickering's anecdotes fit a more parsimonious but overlooked explanation: the quiet seclusion and time for writing available to not only recuperating authors but to many healthy writers as well.

71. Pronzini, B., & Malzberg, B. (1979). Prose bowl. *Fantasy & Science Fiction, 57*, 135-156.

A delightful example of writing problems viewed cynically by science fiction writers. In this futuristic scenario, writing has achieved the spectator appeal and competitiveness accorded to twentieth century football. Rating: PG.

72. Quaytman, W. (1969). Psychotherapist's writing block. *Voices, 4*, 13-17.

In the casual style typical of *Voices*, an in-group journal for psychoanalysts, Quaytman bemoans his writing block of 20 years. Mysteriously cured of blocking, he emphasizes the costs of blocking in failures to communicate vital new ideas and he discounts the arguments he once shared with other cynics–e.g., that too much "crap" is already being published. In a sequel (Ego factors in a psychotherapist's writing block, *Journal of Contemporary Psychotherapy*, 1973, 5, 135-139) inspired by grateful letters from other blocked therapists, Quaytman sounds less positive: writing is difficult and brings delayed rewards, if any, whereas conversation with one's colleagues is both easier and immediately rewarding. Still, he ends on the upbeat in concluding that writers who write are more emotionally integrated than those who want to but don't.

73. Rainer, T. (1978). *The new diary*. Los Angeles: J. P. Tarcher.

A neglected source on programs for blockers, perhaps because it is so directly oriented to women who would keep diaries, Rainer's book teems with useful and interesting ideas. Her approach to unblocking and productivity evolved from free-intuitive writing and emphasizes the safety and freedom of writing, initially at least, away from public scrutiny. In this sense, Rainer's advice amounts to little more than popular free writing techniques. But her experience with writers and their diaries brings insights far beyond those of usual calls to free writing.

74. Ribot, T. (1906). *Essay on the creative imagination*. Chicago: Open Court.

Ribot, a French psychologist, illustrates an attempt to break the myths held by many blockers about the reliance of creativity on sudden inspiration and good luck with assertions like this: "chance is an occasion for, not an agent of, creation" (p. 163). Ribot's relevance for modern work on writing processes and problems including blocking lies in his analysis of mental operations such as dissociation (e.g., simplication of memories), personification (i.e., of inanimate things), and diffluence (i.e., using vague, indistinct images).

75. Rico, G. L. (1983). *Writing the natural way*. Los Angeles: J. P. Tarcher.

At first glance, Rico seems to offer little more than an entertaining application of the fad in speculating about the relevance of split brain mechanisms to writing blocks. Stated briefly, her notion is that natural (i.e., unblocked) writing depends on access to the brain's right hemisphere–the "design mind" with its resources for richness, rhythm, originality, designs, and the inner writer. We get stuck, it follows, when relying too readily on the left hemisphere–the "sign mind" with its predispositions to rational, logical representations and to anxious anticipations of failure. But, the brain metaphors can pay dividends in advice on orchestrating the two hemispheres in tasks like organizing the products of free writing into a clustered outline, in listening for and developing the natural rhythms of a distinctive voice in writing, and in revising by paring for greater economy and craftsmanship. The exercises in the latter part of this book are unique and valuable in directing blockers into activities that transcend and, so, maintain unblocking.

76. Rose, M. (1980). Rigid rules, inflexible plans, and the stifling of language: A cognitive analysis of writer's block. *College Composition and Communication, 31,* 389-401.

In this, and in his dissertation completed a year later (*The cognitive dimension of writer's block*, UCLA), Rose provided the first truly systematic work on blocking by a composition teacher. His premise: rather than asking students if they block, ask them about specific attitudinal processes that may relate to blocking. Rose's sample of freshman composition students indicated that blockers, compared to nonblockers, share qualities including a) shorter drafts, b) more time prewriting and planning, c) premature editing, and d) eight times as many conflicting rules. Indeed, all five of the blockers appeared to use rules (e.g., no-revision strategy) inflexibly and in ways that generally impeded writing.

77. Rose, M. (1985). Complexity, rigor, evolving method, and the puzzle of writer's block: Thoughts on composing-process research. In M. Rose (Ed.), *When a writer can't write* (pp. 227- 260). New York: Guilford.

Here Rose overviews his earlier work on "cognitive" (i.e., the implicit rules used by writers) aspects of blocking. He then conducts a lengthy plea for research on blocking that interweaves cognitive, affective, and situational aspects of writing. Although he posits schemes such as "triangulation" from sociology as a means of establishing a "rigor of multiple sightings rather than a rigor of singular constraints" (p. 229), Rose brings little new clarity or pragmatism to writing blocks here.

78. Rosenberg, M. (1976). Releasing the creative imagination. *Journal of Creative Behavior, 10*, 203-209.

Rosenberg met regularly with student playwrights and established a "hypnotic environment" with convincing suggestions that writing would be easy. Evidently the procedure (which includes strong group support) worked to produce more and freer writing. A follow-up demonstration illustrated the possibilities of using hypnotic suggestion to increase the supply of "raw material" on which writers draw.

79. Rosenberg, H., & Lah, M. I. (1982). A comprehensive behavioral-cognitive treatment of writer's block. *Behavioral Psychotherapy, 10*, 356-363.

This is a single-case study of a graduate student who had procrastinated with his master's thesis. Treatment began with a "task analysis" that indicated a hierarchy of tasks (from least to most difficult) including 1) editing and adding detail and 2) "smoothing." Next, specific ways in which the subject procrastinated were identified (e.g., listening to records). Then, a work schedule was established to reduce the distracting behaviors while rewarding the activities already outlined in the task analysis. Overall, this intervention produced an immediate and consistent increase in "the number of hours of writing, the use of weekdays, and the self-rated effectiveness."

80. Ross, E. I. (1985). *Writing while you sleep . . . and other surprising ways to increase your writing power*. New York: Writers Digest Books.

    Ross takes popularized techniques for unblocking such as guided imagery a step further, into a scheme for gestating writing in the subconscious mind. But she provides little more than admonishment; writers who don't incubate ideas and energy for writing, despite Ross's enthusiastic accounts of what should happen, may remain stuck. And writers may find little solace in repeating maxims 10 times (e.g., "My article is like the coffee ... all the necessary ingredients are simmering in my subconscious mind ... my mind will take the time it needs..."). Instead, they may find they've confirmed their worst suspicions of being beyond help.

81. Roth, P. (1983). *The anatomy lesson*. New York: Farrar, Straus & Giroux.

    In this episode, Nathan Zuckerman (Philip Roth's "alter id") battles disillusionment and blocking ("ten talons clawing at twenty-six letters"):

    > This is not the position in life that I had hoped to fill. I want to be an obstetrician. Who quarrels with an obstetrician? Even the obstetrician who delivered Bugsy Siegel goes to bed at night with a clear conscience. He catches what comes out and every body loves him. When the baby appears they don't start shouting, "You call that a baby? That's not a baby!" No, whatever he hands them, they take it home. They're grateful for his just having been there. (p. 103)

82. Sanavio, E. (1980). A wider model of writer's cramp. *Behavior Analysis & Modification, 4*, 17-27.

    In Europe, compared to America, a common form of writing blocks is writer's cramp (i.e., incoordination and muscular spasms, sometimes a functional paralysis of the hand and arm trying to write). I chose Sanavio's article to represent a surprisingly extensive literature on cramping, over 150 years old, because it provides a broad review of theories and treatments. Two aspects of his review stand out: a) cramped writers tend to be hypertensive, conscientious, and controlled; and b) behavioral treatments employing biofeedback and/or muscular relaxation seem most effective. Authors of articles on writing cramps including Sanavio rarely ascribe relevance to other, less dramatic, forms of blocking or to the complex demands of the writing tasks being avoided.

83. Scanlon, L. (1979). *Writing groups in an interdisciplinary program or getting around the professorial block*. Hartford, CN: Paper presented at the Annual Spring Meeting of the North-East Modern Language Association. (ERIC Document Reproduction Service No. ED 169 546)

Premise: Blocks among students result from competition for grades and the fear/authority carried by teachers. Solution: Writing groups with peer support and evaluation that allow revision and feedback before papers are submitted for grades.

84. Schuman, E. P. (1981). Writing block treated with modern psychoanalytic interventions. *The Psychoanalytic Review, 68*, 113-134.

In fact, Schuman offers nothing very "modern" while leading his readers on a merry chase. First, he lists the failures of his predecessors to help blockers. Then, Schuman speaks at length about the reluctance of therapists to interfere with "lingering" and about issues of transference in general. Thirteen pages later, Schuman finally gets to the maneuver for unblocking his patient: "I asked him, 'Suppose someone said you wouldn't be permitted to write— or submit your dissertation proposal. What would you do?' He became furious. 'I would do it anyway'" (p. 129). By the next session, the patient had written. But Schuman says nothing about the longer run, of whether this patient completed the larger task of writing a dissertation.

85. Sears, P. (1979). *Letter writing: A technique for treating writer's block*. Minneapolis, MN: Paper presented at the Annual Meeting of the Conference on College Composition and Communication. (ERIC Document Reproduction Service No. ED 176 337)

Freshman composition students learned an 11-step process (e.g., select topic, brainstorm it, categorize the details that emerged) to ease writing. Blocked students added a preliminary step: letter writing.

86. Segal, H. (1984). Joseph Conrad and the mid-life crisis. *International Review of Psychoanalysis, 11*, 3-9.

This psychohistory of Conrad focuses on two related principles derived from psychoanalytic speculation. First, the mid-life crisis revives old, unresolved problems such as depressive anxieties and, in turn, mobilizes creative processes such as writing to help express and overcome the malaise. Thus, Conrad at mid-life, having failed to advance to a position of command as a seaman, began to look inward: "I had given myself to the idleness of a haunted man who looks for nothing but words wherein to capture his visions" (p. 4). Second, the mid-life crisis, if unresolved, leads to creative blocking and even an early death.

87. Seidenberg, R. (1961). The concept of lingering. *Psychiatry, 24,* 273-277.

Although Seidenberg does not directly tie the psychoanalytic concept of lingering to blocking, he draws useful parallels such as this:

> The encouraging supervisor, not wanting to interfere with the student's "imaginative" process, fails to give any word of discouragement to such a noble endeavor and allows the candidate to get involved in what turns out to be a design for a perpetual motion machine. (p. 274)

Other lingerers include students who put off dissertations to avoid the responsibilities that accompany the newly won status of Ph.D.

88. Shaughnessy, M. P. (1977). *Errors and expectations.* New York: Oxford University Press.

Mina Shaughnessy's insights into the experience of writing, especially the phenomenology of blocking, are as clear as her writing. Consider her depiction of blocking typical to student writers: "Some writers, inhibited by their fear of error, produce but a few lines an hour or keep trying to begin, crossing out one try after another until the sentence is hopelessly tangled" (p. 7). Shaughnessy shows why feelings of inadequacy are antithetical to the act of confidence and exhibitionism that marks efficient writing (p. 85). And she explains why getting started is the most difficult of all writing problems:

> Without strategies for generating real thought, without an audience he cares to write for, the writer must eke out his first sentence by means of redundancy and digression, strategies that inevitably disengage him from grammatical intuitions as well as his thought. (p. 82)

89. Solomon, L. J., & Rothblum, E. D. (1984). Cognitive-behavioral antecedents of procrastination. *Journal of Counseling Psychology, 31,* 503-509.

This exemplary study of academic procrastination goes beyond traditional considerations (study habits, time management) to other factors that overlap with blocking: evaluation anxiety, difficulty making decisions, lack of assertiveness, fear of success, perfectionism, and perceived aversiveness of the task. A sample of college students produced two main types of procrastinators: the smaller group attributed procrastination to fear of failure. The second group procrastinated because of task aversiveness, although aversiveness was rarely the only reason listed.

90. Sommers, N. (1980). Revision strategies of student writers and experienced adult writers. *College Composition and Communication, 31,* 378-388.

In the midst of a description of mature, experienced writers (i.e., ready and willing to revise in flexible and multiple ways), Sommers offers a brief aside about blocking. Some writers block because the writing process can be threatening: "Good writing disturbs: It creates dissonance. Students need to seek the dissonance of discovery, utilizing in their writing, as the experienced writers do, the very difference between writing and speech—the possibility of revision" (p. 387).

91. Spitzer, R. L. (1980). *Diagnostic and statistical manual of mental disorders* (3rd ed.). Washington, D.C.: American Psychiatric Association.

Is a writing block a mental disorder? In the current edition of the "DSM," the official diagnostic guide for psychiatrists, writing blocks qualify as an "adjustment disorder" (i.e., a pattern of overreaction to an identifiable psychosocial stressor that will eventually remit after the stressor ceases). Specifically:

> *309.23 Adjustment Disorder with Work (or Academic) Inhibition.* This category should be used when the predominant manifestation is an inhibition in work or academic functioning occurring in an individual whose previous work or academic performance has been adequate. Frequently there are also varying mixtures of anxiety and depression. Examples include inability to study and to write papers or reports. (p. 301)

92. Stack, R. (1980). Writing as conversation. *Visible Language, 14,* 376-382.

Critics of research on blocking, especially skeptical journal reviewers, frequently wonder why everyone doesn't assume that blocked writers have nothing to say and, therefore, should be left in peace. Stack's answer:

> Since writing is so patently the property of the powerful, this conviction has the effect of legitimating and perpetuating existing patterns of inequality. We must find a way to give people–people in general, not just the usual select bunch the chance to discover and delight in the power of the word as a mode of self-representation. Writing is the way we make ourselves heard, and if one is not heard, one is unlikely to listen. (p. 379)

93. Suler, J. R. (1980). Primary process thinking and creativity. *Psychological Bulletin, 88,* 144-168.

Suler makes an important and oft-overlooked point; access to creativity via primary-process (i.e., primitive-id) thinking requires a healthy personality. Success in shifting to that level demands a) a secure sense of identity enabling one to cope with illogical and affect-charged aspects of thinking, and b) an interpersonal trust that one's creative work will not necessarily be rejected. Blocking from primary-process thinking may reflect factors such as defiance of authority, a sense of guilt, or a lack of openness to experience.

94. Sulkes, S. (1983). Writer's block–another cause and cure. *Journal of Reading, 26,* 728.

This note adds a point about blocking to Oliver's (1982) earlier assumption that dysfunctional student writers suffer from rigid rules about writing. Sulkes recounts his experiences with student writers who "froze" on assignments. His solution: order them to write a "paper of irredeemable wretchedness." With this assignment the students wrote about their fears of public ridicule and were, presumably, exorcised of their "demons of failure."

95. Upper, D. (1974). An unsuccessful self-treatment of a case of "writer's block." *Journal of Applied Behavior Analysis, 7,* 497.

The format used here to joke about blocking, a title followed by a blank page, has appeared in many journals (e.g., B. P. Hermann, Unsuccessful treatment of a case of writer's block . . . *Perceptual and Motor Skills,* 1984, 58, 350). But Upper's offering has a special significance: It is probably the single best-known article on blocking in psychology.

96. Valian, V. (1977). Learning to work. In S. Ruddick & P. Daniels (Eds.), *Working it out*. New York: Pantheon, 1977.

Valian offers a firsthand account of blocking for other women struggling with work roles in a male-dominated world. Her phenomenological descriptions illustrate how stressful an initial attempt at unblocking can be. She is unusually reflective about her reluctance to write. And, her insight about a curative for blocking is as useful as it is interesting:

> Masters and Johnson's book, *Human Sexual Inadequacy*, gave me the key. In it, Masters and Johnson stressed that sexuality is a natural physiological process with orgasm as a natural end point. They were concerned with the internal roadblocks that prevented full sexual enjoyment. . . therapy took the form of breaking the sexual act down into its components. . . The process was then slowly reassembled, with couples moving on to the next component only after they were comfortable with the preceding one. (p. 165)

97. Walsh, R. (1983). Limits of humanistic psychology: Failure of humanistic psychotherapy to alleviate a case of writer's block occurring as a complication of attempted self-transcendence—a self-report. *Journal of Humanistic Psychology, 23*, 97-98.

This is another in a series of articles whose humor about blocking lies in a title followed by a blank page (see, e.g., Upper, 1974).

98. Wason, P. C. (1980). Conformity and commitment in writing. *Visible Language, 14*, 351-363.

Wason argues that many authors block themselves by assuming that writing should be volitional. The more realistic view of writing is to "exteriorize" some of the responsibility for writing to preparational activities like free writing. The usual problem, in his view, is the reluctance of intellectuals to accept exteriorization because they hold ideals like self-expression too sacrosanct.

99. Weaver, F. S. (1982). Teaching, writing, and developing. *Journal of Higher Education, 53*, 586-592.

Weaver attempts to disarm a common excuse among academicians for not writing: the belief that good teaching and writing are incompatible. His argument: The disciplined efforts necessary to fashion a coherent paper will deepen the teacher's understanding and enjoyment of topics for teaching.

100. Wilkerson, M. (1925). *The way of the makers*. New York: Macmillan.

This delightful compendium of folklore about artistic productivity includes the myth of the inspirational muse . . .

> What can I do in Poetry,
> Now the good Spirit's gone from me?
> Why nothing now, but lonely sit,
> And over-read what I have writ. (Robert Herrick)

and the related myth that writers are incompetent to do more important things:

> Singing is sweet; but be sure of this,
> Lips only sing when they cannot kiss. (James Thomson)

Finding Your Own Voice in Academic Publishing

Writing Your Way to Success

Susan M. Drake & Glen A. Jones

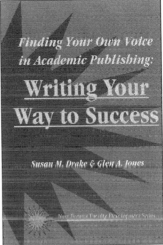

There are many books available that will guide the academic to substantive academic writing. However, approximately 85% of publications are written by 15% of the academic population. Many academics experience the writing process as very difficult and painful, and give up writing rather than try to surmount the obstacles. *Writing Your Way to Success* takes a fresh look at the publishing game and offers tried and true strategies that allowed two new academics to experience publishing success. It certainly will help you too!

Contents Overview

Our Stories – Susan's Writing Path; Glen's Writing Path
Choosing a Focus – Traditional Approaches; Revisiting a Thesis; Working on a Collaborative Project; Action Research; Book Reviews
Finding the Right Journal – Creating a Personalized Data Base; Other Avenues; Rule of Three; Dealing with Rejection
Exploring the Literature – Data Bases; Snowball Approach; Reviewing Systematically; Reviewing With the Computer
Organizing for Clarity – Clarity of Purpose; Editing
And more!

☞ *See last page for ordering information.*

Ideal for Seasoned Profs

STEP by STEP
Building a Research Paper

Patricia M. Shields

Time and organization are two of the biggest obstacles facing students as they begin the process of writing a research paper. *Step-by-Step* transforms "writing a paper" into "organizing a project." This organizer is a versatile tool that helps the student-scholar manage three elements of the term paper assignment: time, materials and ideas. Using the organizer, student-scholars build, make, or do the critical behind-the-scenes elements of writing research papers: manage time, read, think, take notes, make an outline, etc.

STEP by STEP ...
- used by professors to write journal articles
- used by MPA Students for over 10 years
- led to many award winning papers, including the Pi Alpha Alpha award
- adopted in Ph.D. courses
- teaches project management skills
- applied successfully in professional certification programs
- based on John Dewey's "logic of inquiry"

and Grad Students Alike!

What Users Say about Step by Step

STEP by STEP helped me organize the numerous details involved in research that include note taking, important contacts, deadlines, references, and list of things-to-do. It helped me distill the murky sea of information floating through the brainstorming process into a conceptual framework that guided the focus of my research.

Shivaun Perez, Education Policy Consultant
Winner 2000 Pi Alpha Alpha Master's Student Paper Award

I have written a number of research projects over the years and still have vivid memories of scattered note cards, misplaced articles, overdue library books, scribbled legal pads and lost ideas. Indeed, there is nothing worse than an 11th-hour search for that perfect citation... "Where did I put that article!?" Dr. Shields' step-by step approach to building a research project eliminates all that confusion, and in its place provides a sequential, logical and structured process for conducting and organizing research. What's more, this practical approach to research provides a critical forum for internal debate ... an opportunity to write and think about what we have read and to link our analysis to personal experience.

Kevin L. Baum, Austin Fire Department Battalion Chief
Winner 1998 Pi Alpha Alpha Master's Student Paper Award

In addition to assisting the student in organizing his or her project, Step-by-Step stimulates fertile and productive thinking in a critical manner.

Sam Wilson, Bluebonnet Community Mental Health Center

STEP by STEP allowed me to keep all relevant materials in one place. I could easily pick up where I had left off.

Patricia Hicks, Chief of Staff, Texas Lieutenant Governor

STEP by STEP is an important tool against the battle of procrastination.

David Rejino, Texas A&M University System

The *STEP by STEP* method allowed me to see specific patterns in the literature.

Ralph E. Revello, Hospital Administrator
Winner 1997 Research Award, Centex ASPA

 See last page for ordering information.